PRAISE FOR
Manager's M

"Manager's Mentor gives excellent management ideas based on actual experiences in starting and running a company. You can't beat that kind of advice."
— FLOYD E. OLSON
43 years managing small and large companies

"What a marvelous book! With warm, engaging stories, Ron Parks has illustrated solid principles of commerce and management. This is the best business book I've read."
— DENNIS ROURKE
Director of Risk Management, First Data Corp.
Author of *The Lost Art of Human Memory*

"No gimmicks or useless generalities here. This is a long-term, strategic approach to business management. *Manager's Mentor* is full of specific, practical advice — but more than that, it shows how to think through the myriad issues of running a business. No book can provide all the answers, but *Manager's Mentor* shows how to ask the right questions."
— DAVID BRISTOW
Managing Editor, *Nebraska Life*

"I was told early on that, if I wanted to be successful, I should find someone else who is and do what they do. Ron Park's book introduced me to a successful mentor whom I could consult from my chair at home. He clearly answered important questions that, due to my lack of experience, I wouldn't have even thought to ask. The pages are filled with practical advice that has helped me build for the future, as well as avoid costly mistakes in the present. As a result, my two-year-old business is off to a great start."
— JAMES P. SCHOLZ
President, Scholz Images

"I'd been a small-business owner for 28 years before reading Ron Parks's book. It enlightened me to pay closer attention to many costs and details I wasn't aware of as part of my cost of production. I especially enjoyed the book's entertaining format and Ron's delightful short-story examples."

– MARY ANNE VACCARO
Clothing designer and manufacturer

"Ron Parks, with his journalist-wife Judith, paints his picture with all the poignancy of Willa Cather's *One of Ours* and Mari Sandoz's *The Cattleman*, splashed in the splendid melody of Nebraska's legendary poet laureate, John G. Neihardt. *Manager's Mentor* is more than a candidate for one of Donald R. Hickey's 'Nebraska Moments' – it is a monument, a legacy, to Nebraska's pioneers, a guiding light to those who dare."

– GLENN E. DAVIS
Nebraska Director
U.S. Small Business Administration

"Ron Parks and his wife, Judith, with her considerable skills in communication, share what he has learned by providing a book that is easy to read and much needed in the world of business. *Manager's Mentor* illustrates that, even in business, successful living involves the moral values that have come to be associated with integrity."

– VERNON G. GOFF, B.A., Th.M., D.Min.
Author of *Making God Talk Make Sense*

"Right from the start, I enjoyed reading *Manager's Mentor*. It's given me a better understanding of the influences and ideas behind good management decisions so, although I work for a large company rather than a small one, I've become a better manager – and a better-informed employee."

– RICHARD L. STOLZ
Senior Accountant, Expense Analyst
Safeco Life Insurance Company

Manager's Mentor

A GUIDE FOR SMALL BUSINESS

Manager's Mentor

A GUIDE FOR SMALL BUSINESS

RONALD K. PARKS
as told to JUDITH STOLZ PARKS

Foreword by ROBERT E. BERNIER, Ph.D.

Prairie Sky Publishing Company
Omaha, Nebraska

Published by Prairie Sky Publishing Company
P.O. Box 45083, Omaha, Nebraska 68145-0083

Printed and bound in the United States of America

Printed by BookMasters, Inc., Mansfield, Ohio
Book Designer: Steve Raglin, Omaha, Nebraska
Fonts: Adobe Garamond, Bodoni, and Futura
Cover stock: Carolina Cover, 12 point, coated one side
Inside pages stock: Natural Glatfelter, 60# text

Parks, Ronald K.; 1939-
    Manager's mentor : a guide for small business /
  Ronald K. Parks as told to Judith Stolz Parks ; foreword
  by Robert E. Bernier
    p. cm.
    Includes index.
    LCCN 2003102898
    ISBN 0-9729165-0-4

    1. Small business--Management.   I. Parks, Judith
  Stolz.   II. Title.

  HD62.7.P375 2003   658.02'2
                            QBI03-200235

For ordering information and to provide feedback, ask questions, and make suggestions for the next edition, please write to the publisher or visit our website: www.managersmentor.com.

To Wayne and Hazel Parks
My parents, who gave me unflagging support all their lives

To Jay Quick
My accountant and dear friend, who gave me invaluable guidance

Contents

Foreword

There is more than one kind of small business and more than one kind of small-business owner. That is why this book by Ron and Judy Parks is so valuable. That may seem, once you read *Manager's Mentor*, an ironic statement because this book is about a particular kind of small business and a particular kind of small-business owner. I make it because Ron Parks is the kind of small-business owner-manager often ignored in books and articles about small business, whether they are popular or academic. And yet, small-business owners in the mold of Ron Parks are the kind that build solid companies, provide dependable employment, and are the foundation of good communities.

Two kinds of small-business owners are focused on in public policy. The most often talked about are those engaged in attempting to build a large business. They are lionized as creative risk takers who are the champions of capitalism. The most successful become darlings of the media – Bill Gates and Steve Jobs, for example. Most who attempt such ventures are unsuccessful, but that only serves to make more attractive those who are. The other kind of small business, commonly understood, is the self-employment business – often called the "Mom and Pop business." This kind may have a handful of employees, especially part-time employees, but does not grow. Self-employment businesses are viewed as benefiting from rather than contributing to economic growth. And subject to pressures from larger and more sophisticated companies, their survival becomes questionable.

Such a dichotomous view of small business obscures the kind discussed in this book. Yet, such businesses exist in virtually every substantial community. They are the small businesses that find and exploit profitable markets, obtain modest but sustained growth, and employ people in substantial jobs. They are often successful over a long period of time. Thus, they provide stable employment. And many of them engage in "primary" industries. That is, their customer base is largely outside the community they reside in, so their sales bring money into the community. Theirs is the kind of business that means economic vitality. Such a situation is different from that of "secondary" businesses (usually retail), which circulate money within a community.

Academic study of small businesses is only about forty years old. Most of the early research focused on what characteristics were common among those bold enough to start their own business. That research has been spectacularly unsuccessful. That is not to say that individuals do not possess certain characteristics that help them perform better as entrepreneurs than other individuals. It is to say that entrepreneurship is a process and that learning the process is as important as natural ability. It is like saying there are no great baseball players in Finland. It isn't that no one in Finland has the natural ability to play baseball. It is that baseball is a game foreign to Finland. There are no baseball heroes to emulate or coaches to teach you the game.

In the game of entrepreneurship, Ron Parks is a major league player. By reading this book you will get insights and examples available few other places. In reading his stories about life on the farm while growing up, I am reminded of the television commercials for an investment banking firm. Each of them shows a common enough event watching a foreign movie or playing a bagpipe – and then asks the question "What lessons can we learn?" It then draws from the event a lesson about life and investment. It ends with the tagline, "Wisdom is everywhere. Uncommon wisdom is knowing where to find it." It is that kind of uncommon wisdom you will find in the lessons Ron Parks draws from his experiences as a boy.

Some things stand out in this book, at least to me. Some stand out because they confirm things most small-business consultants have always thought about entrepreneurship. Others stand out because they run counter to accepted wisdom.

You will find here the story of a man who grew up loving machinery and who worked for others before striking out on his own. This confirms the idea that an entrepreneur should do that which he knows and loves. Someone who begins a business only with the idea of making money risks failing to stay with the business long enough and with enough commitment to make it a success. After all, there isn't any sense in making for yourself a job you won't like.

To make for yourself a job also implies you are the boss, and that is a significant lure of small-business ownership. What you will learn in this book is that it isn't enough to want to be your own boss if you do not bring to the task a strong set of values. Ron Parks expresses very strong values in this book about high standards, community involvement, selection and treatment of customers, selection and treatment of employees, training of employees, investment in capital equipment, and many other aspects of small-business management. I liked especially his spirited defense of the time card as an equitable and just system for both employer and employee. More important than the specific recommendations themselves is the reasoned conviction with which Ron Parks reached his positions on business management. No one wants to work for someone who is arbitrary and capricious, even if that person is yourself.

Through the sound presentation of ideas steeped in experience and reason, Ron Parks presents himself as he claims in the title – a mentor. If you are a small-business owner or you have aspirations of small-business ownership and are looking for a successful hero and model to emulate, you have picked the right book.

– ROBERT E. BERNIER, Ph.D.
  Assistant Dean, College of Business Administration
  State Director, Nebraska Business Development Center
  University of Nebraska at Omaha

What Makes This Book Unique

As a kid on a farm in the Nebraska Sand Hills, I decided early on I didn't want to be a farmer when I grew up. Instead, since 1972 I've owned and managed a stainless-steel fabricating company in Omaha, Nebraska. We design and make equipment for the food-processing industry – chicken cookers the size of boxcars, for instance, and convoluted conveyor systems as long as a football field.

Through 30 years of roller-coaster business cycles, I've never laid off a worker for economic reasons, despite substantial short-term losses. My employees and I have grown the company from $250,000 in sales to nearly $10 million today. Our annualized average rate of turnover for fulltime employees is eight percent. And we've developed a standard-setting, state-of-the-art operation in an industry in which workers' compensation claims are expected and visits from representatives of the Occupational Safety and Health Administration (OSHA) feared.

I learned a lot about managing the challenges and responsibilities of running a business, as a member of a family eking out a living during the shortages brought on by the Great Depression and World War II. I've learned a lot more owning and running my company.

So my wife, Judith, and I have written *Manager's Mentor: A Guide for Small Business* to help others gain from my experiences and avoid my mistakes. It's for both the doers and the dreamers – those who already own or manage a small business and those who are thinking about either prospect. It provides an insider's insight, from someone who actually runs a company; reading it will help you gain additional business wisdom.

To say writing this book was a labor of love might sound trite, but I mean it. I love capitalism and free enterprise. However flawed it is, our economic system is still the best in the world. It provides a setting in which we can chase and fulfill our dreams, provide for our family, and give others a means to earn a living. Here we can conquer new challenges and grow in ability and responsibility. And we can get ahead enough to give to others who are less blessed and to the community for the greater good.

I especially love small business, which generates most of the steam that keeps our great economic system running. According to the Small Business Administration (SBA), small businesses constitute 99 percent of the country's employers. They create two of every three new jobs.

In 2000 alone, 612,400 new small firms opened, says the SBA, joining the other approximately six million chugging along. It's no surprise, then, that small-business development centers, business-incubator programs, training seminars, consultants, magazines, newsletters, and, yes, books are proliferating. People want – and need – to know how to make their enterprise succeed.

Many books on the market purport to be the complete guide to starting and running a business. Nonsense. No single book can be that comprehensive. The smart individual reads across the spectrum and incorporates ideas from many sources, including, I hope, this one.

Acknowledgments

This book happened because of the dedication, hard work, and support of many people. My children, Wes and Vicki, encouraged me. Other family members, my friends, business associates, and colleagues prompted me to talk about my ideas and willingly listened. My wife, Judith, companion in the adventures of life and collaborator on this and many other projects, engaged me in conversations about business for years before we got serious about writing this book. I thank her, especially, for her endless support and love.

My employees, with their broad expertise, continuous effort, support, and friendship through thick and thin, have made the challenges easier to bear and the many accomplishments we've had wonderful to share. I thank them for all they've taught me and for all they've done for me. The company is successful because of them.

I also thank everyone who has supported us in this endeavor, especially our manuscript readers, who were so generous with their time. Their suggestions and welcome scrutiny helped clarify my message and keep me on track. Any errors are mine.

Introduction

Consider the man with a sprained ankle who, when the emergency-room nurse asked if he knew how to use crutches, answered, "Yeah, sure," and took the pair she offered him. He put one foot forward and fell on his face. "I thought you said you could use crutches!" the nurse exclaimed. His answer: "Well, I've watched other people using them and it didn't look hard."

Before they start, many business dreamers think running a business looks easy. Indeed, the naive onlooker's view is like the satellite image of a hurricane: deceptively and beautifully simple. But managing the countless details of a business might make one think surviving a hurricane would be easier.

All the daily pressures are difficult enough. Add to them the constant awareness that success or failure affects not just the owner or manager but also the employees – and their families. Well, such responsibility is not for the faint of heart or the unprepared.

While more than half a million businesses were opening in 2000 with enthusiasm and high hopes, 234,300 others had to close, according to the Small Business Administration (SBA), because of reasons as varied as the businesses themselves. Inadequate cash flow, poor employee-management, and too many inefficiencies are but three of the pitfalls. To see one's business fail after putting in the long hours, hard work, and worry, not to mention money, counts among life's biggest heartbreaks.

Manager's Mentor: A Guide for Small Business will help the reader avoid that heartbreak. Based on my 30 years as owner and manager of a small business recognized for quality and achievement in its industry, this book explains the principles, and their practical applications, that have helped me develop good business sense and guided me toward successful decisions.

My rural memories, featured in "A Sand Hills Farm Education" and in vignettes at the opening of each chapter, are in this book because our family farm was the training ground for my business success. There I learned many of the values, thought processes, and strategies that have served me well and that I share with you in the pages that follow.

A note of caution for the gender-sensitive: My industry, manufacturing, still tends to be mostly male, and Judith, my wife, who put my ideas on paper, thinks "his or her" phrasing is awkward. So except for the clear references to women, this book is written in the masculine gender. We hope you'll overlook that nod to traditionalism and attend to the message.

We've done the easy part. The hard part – thinking – is up to you, as you consider the information and decide how to apply it to your circumstances.

A Sand Hills Farm Education

I was born in 1939, 10 years after the stock-market crash of October 1929. The Great Depression still lingered for many families, especially farm families such as mine. My father had sold his share in a tractor and a corn picker when he moved from his first farm to the one on which I grew up in Pierce County, Nebraska. Unable to buy such big equipment on his own and with no farmers in the area willing to invest with him, for years he was forced to use horse-drawn equipment.

Until I was five or six, we had no hot water, no electricity, and no indoor toilet. We cooked on a wood-burning stove and used kerosene lanterns. We had an outdoor john; toilet paper was a *Sears & Roebuck* catalog. A stand-alone kerosene stove in the living room heated the entire two-story house, and not very well at that, without wall insulation. The walls had so many leaks that, during windstorms, dust blew into the house.

Until my older brother, Nelson, left home, I shared a bed with him. Then my brother Merle, younger by seven years, took his place. Aside from the bed, our bedroom furniture was two upended orange crates with flour sacks strung across the open side. Many years later, at a ranch sale, Mom and Dad bought me a dresser for $5. I still have it.

Learning About Work

One of my earliest recollections is of riding to the field with Mom and Dad in a wagon drawn by our team of horses, Flossie and Fanny. Bundled in a specially built box in the wagon bed, I watched as my parents shucked ears of corn and threw them into the wagon.

In my folks' estimation, learning to walk meant I could start doing chores. I became a "gofer," (go for this and go for that) and my apprenticeship began.

When Dad fixed fence, I, at age three or four, was along to carry his hammer for him and fetch whatever he needed. Thus, at an early age, I started learning the names and uses of tools.

No job was too small for a little kid. I fetched jars from the cellar and popcorn ears, air-dried, from the attic; hauled bushel baskets of cobs and armloads of wood for the cook stove and the heating stove; planted seeds in the melon patch and the garden and the corn plot; gathered and wrapped apples in catalog pages to put in the storage barrel; helped with washing clothes and hanging them up to dry.

At about the age of six, I began helping the threshing crews, though not in the way I'd hoped – that is, working with the men. My job was to catch – and kill – a dozen free-range chickens for the crew's lunch. I would run through the woods and around the farm trying to corner and catch those chickens any way I could.

You can imagine a kid of six or seven trying to hold on to a desperate rooster and wring its neck. As Dad explained, "You have to break that blood vessel in the neck. You have to twist off that head so it'll bleed." This was work for somebody much bigger and stronger. But one way or another, those poor chickens were butchered.

Today, my company makes poultry-processing equipment. It's a lot easier than chasing down free-range chickens and engaging them in their life-or-death struggle.

Like other farm kids, I grew up around machinery and tools. I used hammers, saws, pipe wrenches, crescent wrenches, socket wrenches. I wasn't playing or pretending; we were doing real jobs that had to be done, because we had to get into the fields.

Dad didn't give much instruction. Most of the time, he'd just walk by something and tell me to take care of it. I had to figure out how to do the project, so I learned by trial and error and, mostly, by watching my parents.

For example, Dad would walk around the cultivator, pointing out the shoe blades he wanted changed, and I would have to figure out how to change them. Bloody fingers sometimes were a byproduct of the job. During combining season, when he came in for lunch, he'd have me grease all the zerks, or grease fittings, on the combine.

There were about 45 of them, some in hard-to-reach places. Many were on a shaft that had to be turned. I'd squeeze the trigger of the grease gun until I thought my hands were going to fall apart. Then Dad would have me redo the ones I didn't fill right the first time. Probably the easiest of my equipment chores was servicing the tractors with gasoline and water. For a kid nine or 10 years old, that, too, was a big responsibility.

When our folks didn't need our help, we got to play, but we'd better not be out of earshot. We were always on call.

Learning How to Make Money

We kids didn't know what allowances were. When we went to town, we might get a nickel for an ice cream cone. Dad didn't tell me I was doing a good job, and he didn't make me feel I was doing him any favors. Most farm kids did the same kind of work.

But I figured out early how to make some extra money. For instance, a rancher for whom I worked gave me a runt pig. I fed it whole milk, not the skim milk the other pigs were getting, and soon it wasn't a runt anymore. When I sold that pig, I got $65 for it, a lot of money in those days.

I also raised calves for 4-H. Because Dad insisted I put the sale money into a bank account, I had enough money when I was 15 to buy my own car.

Learning About the Real World

After a stint in the Navy, I attended junior college for a short time, then returned to the farm to see about working with Dad. But that prospect didn't work and I left for Florida, where a job awaited me. I didn't make it. A car wreck stranded me in Omaha. I had $20 in my pocket.

While I waited to pick up the insurance check for my car, I was hired at a local manufacturing company for $1.25 an hour. During the next four years, I advanced within the shop, but I was always bored. To make my job more challenging and interesting, I looked for ways to enhance quality control and to improve efficiency. I even became a liaison between the company and the university to organize a college-rebate program for employees.

I was doing good things for my department, but not until I decided to quit did management invite me to go into a foreman-training program. By then, it was too late; I already knew staying there wasn't the best thing for me.

Looking for Learning

I was looking for a job, but I wasn't looking for just a paycheck. I wanted a training opportunity, a situation that would give me solid experiences for the future. I saw an ad in the paper for a job at a steel-fabrication company in Omaha and obtained an interview through a local employment agency.

As I walked through the company shop, I saw big machines, trucks, railroad cars full of steel. It was Heaven. I thought, "This is where I want to be."

The minute I walked into the interview, I started asking questions. Several other men had applied, but I got the job. When I asked the bosses later why they had picked me, they said, "Because you asked the questions that should have been asked." I started as a shop trainee at $2.50 an hour. It wasn't good pay, but I didn't care about the wage; I cared about what I was going to be able to learn.

I enjoyed my work at that company. Unlike a lot of my work on the farm, it wasn't procedural. We always were building something different. I learned how to do custom metalworking and found I liked it. With the permission of my employers, I started my own metal-working company on the side to help with projects they couldn't do.

I stayed with my employers five years, until my own company grew large enough to require my full attention. Business was so good that, in a scramble for new accommodations, I bought an existing manufacturing company.

Applying My Education

When I took over the company, we had 13 employees and assets of about $85,000: $25,000 in inventory and $60,000 in equipment. Much of the equipment, its technology predating World War II, was worn and badly needed to be replaced. I worked weekends on extra jobs to finance new machines, and I filled my new building with machinery.

A tornado destroyed the roof in 1975, causing $50,000 in damages. We took this opportunity to expand to 18,000 square feet. In doing so, we were able to accommodate another new piece of equipment that cost more than twice the assets of the entire company. Through several expansions between then and now, including a new building, we've grown to 110,000 square feet.

As a farm kid, I couldn't even imagine this situation, but looking back on my life, I can see how my experiences and my choices led me to it.

PART I

Getting Started

Chapter 1
Should You Be In Business?

As a farm kid, I was around business activities all the time. We were buying and selling cattle, raising and selling grain, buying and maintaining equipment, working with tools and heavy machinery, managing inventories of livestock and farm products, converting goods by feeding grain to fatten out cattle, adding value to products such as the certified vetch seed we sold. With responsibilities beyond what most city kids had, I learned to be resourceful and self-sufficient.

I grew up with the idea I could take care of myself. So when I thought about what I was going to do for the rest of my life, I thought about doing something where I was in charge of my work.

When I graduated from high school, I needed to get away from the farm, see the world, have a change of scenery. I joined the Navy and, with advanced training, became an aviation machinist's mate. But I disliked that trade. The work was repetitive, like going up and down the cornrows, a job I'd hated on the farm. Had I stayed with it, I'd have become a specialty leader, perhaps an expert on props, with the prestige attached to that position.

Instead, I finished my tour of duty supervising a crew who took care of all the planes before and after maintenance. I was doing a job requiring less training but offering a higher quality of life, with more time off. As a youngster with the beaches nearby, an afternoon at the water was a lot more fun than tearing a cylinder off an airplane engine.

I was discharged early to go to college, but it wasn't for me. I was four years older than my classmates, and my stint in the Navy had widened the gap between us. Instead, I returned to the farm. Egg-laying as an industry was just beginning in Nebraska, and Dad figured he could make good money at it. We planned to go into business together.

But Mom wanted none of it, and to keep peace in the family, I left home again.

I worked at small and major manufacturing corporations. In the process, I realized that the quest to be in business for myself had never gone away. Slowly, by working for other people, I found the things that went back to my farm roots. I'd always enjoyed working with machinery and designing ways to do and make things. My custom manufacturing business is an extension of what I'd done since I was a child.

The Prospect of Running a Business

Being a business owner is an itch that can't be scratched any other way. It's the kind of itch that drives people who succeed at becoming an actor or a singer or an astronaut. Such people have a dream, and they go after it however they can. That's the kind of determination success in business requires. If you don't have it, you won't be able to stick out the tough times.

You probably won't get the itch from taking business classes. Academia can prepare you for positions, but it won't necessarily turn you into a successful entrepreneur. It can't provide you with the necessary commitment and energy. Only you can do that. It can't give you the personality traits that most successful entrepreneurs have in common. Can it help you make the right choice? Perhaps.

Wrong Reasons

It is in buying or starting a business that ill-prepared business seekers are most apt to make their first serious misstep. If the prospect of owning a business seems inviting, consider why it appeals to you. Weed your criteria for determining whether to go into business. The wrong reasons will start you on a long, agonizing course of frustration and disappointment. Here are four wrong reasons:

WRONG REASON NO. 1: I want to be my own boss.

Fine. But do you really think you won't have to answer to anybody when you own a business? Let me give you just a short list of those who will be demanding (notice I did not say "requesting") your time, knocking at your door, breathing down your neck, or threatening to otherwise unbalance your blissful state of mind: investors; government agencies, federal, state, and local; insurance companies; the bank; your employees; your customers; your vendors; and charitable organizations expecting your support, to name just a few.

And no, you won't be able to call your own shots, unless you are realistic enough to interpret that phrase as having some choice about which problems and emergencies you will address in your 12-hour, 15-hour, or 18-hour regular workday. In other words, being your own boss doesn't mean you get more time off; it usually means you work longer hours and so you may get less per hour than you pay your employees.

WRONG REASON NO. 2: I don't want to be making money for somebody else.

That's an uncharitable attitude. Be thankful you can make money for somebody else, because at least you're proving your skills are marketable. And you're taking home an income that may be more than the owner takes home after the company bills are paid. If your employer does make more than you, well, isn't that the way it's supposed to be? After all, he is shouldering all the burdens you don't know about (yet).

Being an indispensable employee for someone else is great practice for owning your own business.

WRONG REASON NO. 3: This is the only chance I'll get to buy (or start) a business.

Nonsense. Nothing will get you into hot water faster than impatience. This is not a matter of jumping at an opportunity; this is a matter of self-discipline. Take your time to analyze the situation carefully so you can avoid the misery that accompanies a silly decision. Don't assume you'll work everything out once you own the business. You won't.

WRONG REASON NO. 4: Owning a business will enhance my self-esteem (or give me better standing in the community or some other version of such an idea).

This may not even be a conscious thought, but that doesn't make it any less dangerous. Owning a business requires a commitment far beyond what one sees from the outside, a commitment that comes from a strong sense of purpose. If the only reason you're going into business is to feel better about yourself, you'd be better off spending your money on a good therapist.

Entrepreneurial Traits

Many entrepreneurs, whose imagination has gotten the better of them, would summarize their business ventures this way: "If I had known what I was getting into before I started this, I never would have tried it." Sometimes our dreams get us into trouble.

But our dreams also keep us plodding until we at last get out of it. In the long run, many entrepreneurs, including me, are glad they chased their dream, and their success and satisfaction refute any doubts they made a good choice.

The very definition of "entrepreneur," according to *Webster's New World Dictionary*, is "a person who organizes and manages a business undertaking, assuming the risk for the sake of the profit." There you have it: risk taking is a vital characteristic of a successful business owner. Even owning a franchise, which is less risky than a start-up, is riskier than working for someone else.

I left my first manufacturing job because I realized good pay and good benefits were keeping me in a boring and unpromising situation. I had confidence that, with my skills, I could and would replace my salary. Some of my fellow workers intoned, "Ron, you're making a terrible mistake. You shouldn't quit a job like this, because the pay and benefits are so good."

But I saw that intelligent, able people could be enticed into doing something far below their capability, because of one thing: security. Yet when the company downsized, many of those who worried about my security lost their own jobs.

That event taught me if I didn't risk, I couldn't succeed. I don't mean taking just any risk; that's mere foolhardiness. I mean taking calculated risks, where the possibility of success is greater than the possibility of failure. If I don't take reasonable chances, I don't get to explore possibilities and options. For me, life is about trying new things.

The Critical Triad

The willingness to accept risk for profit is fundamental to being an entrepreneur. Let's look at some other important qualities. In particular, there are three attributes a person must have not only to get into a business situation but also to stick it out. The first is the ability to learn quickly.

Entrepreneurs typically don't have all the facts before they launch a business, but their dream of success, their determination, and their enthusiasm override their lack of information. Nevertheless, if they are to succeed, they overcome their ignorance in a hurry. Successful entrepreneurs are quick studies.

They also learn enough to figure out when the business is more than they'll ever be able to handle, so they can determine when they'd best get out rather than stubbornly drive their company into the ground.

Those so ignorant they don't know what they don't know are doomed. Your business won't last if you don't recognize how the changing demands of an evolving marketplace affect it. How many buggy manufacturers are still in the transportation-equipment industry today?

The next required quality is pride. I don't mean arrogance but, rather, a strong ego. Put another way, you're so proud you won't admit you were naive enough to get involved in your venture in the first place, so you keep going. You don't admit (except to yourself) you don't know enough; you just keep trying to fill in the blanks of your ignorance until you've learned what you need to know.

Successful business owners believe in themselves. They have confidence. They are convinced the world will appreciate their business, they can contribute, they will succeed.

But pride can sabotage you if you won't admit a project is an inappropriate one for your company and you should get out of it, or if you go into debt too deeply to recover because you refuse to admit defeat at all costs.

The third quality of this critical triad is tenacity. Tenacity gets you through the low spots, when ignorance has you reeling from your mistakes and pride is seeping away. A stubborn refusal to quit makes successful entrepreneurs slog along, one foot in front of the other, until they come through the quagmire of their difficulties – as long as they have the ability to recognize their realistic limits before they get in over their head.

Other Personality Tendencies

Hard times will occur, so a tolerance for adversity is an important consideration for an individual looking into buying a business or starting one. Of course, the accompanying consideration is how much risk and adversity the individual's family can tolerate.

A good possibility exists that the lifestyle will backslide and that little perks to which everyone is accustomed will have to be put on hold. Can the family stand eating out less, canceling a vacation, or fixing up the old car rather than buying a new one? If the word is "yes," then the potential owner has passed "Go" and gets to collect $200.

As I was first growing my business, whenever I'd buy a machine, I'd say, "Well, that's my cabin on the river," or "This is the nicest boat." My friends in jobs paying good money were buying such things, but those wonderful enhancements weren't serious options for me. Though

I made sure my family had the things they really needed and wanted, when the early choices were between the business and the frills, I chose the business, because as it grew, our lifestyle correspondingly improved.

In addition to the critical triad and a high tolerance for risk and adversity, some other personality tendencies seem to suit a person for success as an entrepreneur. For example, being proactive rather than reactive – taking matters into one's own hands rather than waiting for something to happen – seems to bode well for a business owner. A person who leans toward proactivity is in a good frame of mind to take responsibility when necessary. Business owners do that – a lot.

Another characteristic that seems to go with proactivity is the quest for attainment. People who enjoy setting and achieving goals have an advantage in starting a business, because they have the drive and commitment necessary for success.

Successful business managers tend to be generalists; they tend to look at the big picture, rather than concentrate on the details. In an extreme description, a generalist "jumps from mountaintop to mountaintop"; a specific, on the other hand, is compelled to look at every stone on each mountain.

You might ask, "Isn't attention to details important?" Of course it is, but running a business, even running a department within a business, requires the ability to address all the many issues affecting your operation. A manager who focuses on the details won't have time to get to everything that demands attention. In fact, he might not even notice that, while he's concentrating on accounting calculations, the roof is leaking and the second-to-last employee just quit.

The best way for a manager to attend to the details is to delegate them. Hire an accountant to mind the bookkeeping minutiae and report the results to you, for example. It seems to be easier for a generalist to delegate the details than for someone who's detail-oriented to delegate the overseeing duties.

A good business leader is both inclusionary and exclusionary. Being inclusionary, that is, liking people and looking for reasons to include them or to incorporate ideas is important, because so much of business is about working with others. At the same time, being exclusionary, that is, more cautious, more likely to look for the negative side of a person or a situation, is necessary, because it provides the skepticism that prevents one from taking things at face value and getting blindsided. It prods one to set criteria for selecting employees, to establish progress checkpoints, to inspect for quality.

Being too inclusive results from unbridled optimism, the notion that nothing bad will happen. It gets businesses into trouble, because of course things go wrong. The economy drops. Employees go to work for competitors. Suppliers go out of business.

And being too exclusive, requiring extra proof someone or something is acceptable, is harmful, too. Obvious suspicion alienates people who otherwise would be supporters or team members. I once had a supervisor whose idea of a compliment was: "Well, you didn't screw that up." Who wants to follow a leader like that?

A healthy dose of realism helps balance either approach. It is hard enough to see things as they are rather than as we wish – or fear – them to be, but the person who can gather and face the facts is in a better position to decide about any situation than one whose thinking is romantic, subjective, or wishfully idealistic. A person inclined to carefully think before deciding about a situation is more likely to be a successful entrepreneur than a person who reacts emotionally.

A person who thinks for himself might be a good entrepreneur. Having one's own philosophy and goals, rather than looking to others for what to do, bodes well for the person who wants to run a business. Starting or running a business requires someone who isn't afraid of being in charge and who has ideas of his own. Otherwise, he would be content working for someone else who has the ideas.

A preference to look for options rather than follow someone else's procedures is important. An "options" person facing a problem will look for many possible solutions, whereas a "procedures" person will want to know what process to follow to solve the problem or will jump at the first idea that comes to mind if a procedure doesn't exist.

An options person likely would be happier starting up or buying an independent business. A procedures person, on the other hand, might find more fulfillment operating a franchise operation, where processes already are spelled out and where oversight is provided by franchise representatives.

Similarly, entrepreneurs enjoy change. Starting a business is about change: new opportunities, new problems, new situations every day. Someone who wants things to stay the same wouldn't be able to keep up with all those interesting and challenging demands, nor would he likely enjoy all the commotion.

Personality traits affect our success and happiness in all areas of life, especially our occupations, where we spend so much of our time. I've outlined here the traits I think pertain most strongly to success as an entrepreneur. In chapter 8, "Insight," you'll read about personality traits and the importance of matching employees' personalities with job requirements.

Before You Jump

If you think you have a good chance of succeeding as an entrepreneur, you can stack the odds in your favor by considering these issues as you prepare to own a business.

Choose Right

First of all, you should be proud to be in the business you've chosen. You should believe being in that business will give you satisfaction. For instance, I like to stand back and look at products I've built, so I decided long ago I would rather work at creating tangibles and capital goods than something that would be thrown away after one use.

Another factor to consider is how much you like to be with people. Many of us enjoy the camaraderie of a small organization. The group gets to be rather like a family, but you had better like interacting daily with "brothers" and "sisters."

And consider the kind of people with whom you like to work. I like the shop setting, and I like people who have high standards. I certainly am not looking for mavericks or rebels or individualists or any other characters for whom self-expression is the ultimate ambition. I prefer people who cooperate with others on a team. I also know I would much rather work with industrial customers than retail customers.

You gain a huge advantage by focusing on an industry about which you know something. By the time the company I bought came into my line of vision, I had worked for a steel company for several years, and I had started a metalworking job shop as a part-time enterprise.

If, instead, you choose an unfamiliar industry, your learning curve might be so steep that by the time you've learned what you need to know to succeed, your company is bankrupt.

Being familiar with an industry – more than that, knowing an industry – makes you aware of such important aspects as the profit potential, the strength of the marketplace, product costs, distribution sources, staffing requirements, purchasing needs, and networking with people valuable to your selected industry.

Many people who go into the steel industry, for example, don't know even the basic function of how to buy steel competitively. Right there, they've tied their ankles together in the marketplace competition.

If a particular business interests you, but you don't know anything about the industry it's in, do whatever you have to do to learn before you buy the company. Take classes that pertain to the industry. Read the trade magazines, a great educational resource. Get a job with a company similar to the one you want to own, and learn as an employee about all the aspects of running it. That is, work for somebody who's already doing what you think you want to do.

If you confirm that, indeed, this is the kind of business in which you want to be, the experience you gain as an employee will be valuable beyond measure as you proceed with your own company-ownership goals.

On the other hand, if you learn you don't fit in the industry, think of what you've saved yourself in costs and misery by not trying to run your own business before learning the necessities.

Consider what you can and can't do financially. The saying "A sale can be consummated only when there is a willing seller and a willing buyer" doesn't go far enough. Where buying businesses is concerned, willing buyers may be swarming, but they may not be qualified. That is, they may not have the financial strength to carry them through the purchase and the tumultuous early years.

If you don't look like you can make a go of it, financial institutions won't lend you money, and a seller financing a portion of the sale of his business isn't likely to sell to you. A smart seller sets minimum criteria for the buyer's ability to buy.

Frankly, I wasn't a financially strong buyer nor an experienced one for the original owner of my company. I wouldn't have sold to me. But he thought I could manage the business. The bank gave me a loan, because the owner agreed to let the bank have the first mortgage on the equipment. The bank also gave me a $30,000 line of credit, because the owner agreed to give me 10 years to buy the company.

Practice First

Before you take the entrepreneurial plunge, you can get some idea of whether you have the ability to think in entrepreneurial terms by working for someone else. Forget about salary; you want experience and knowledge. You want to learn to identify problems and organize solutions like a manager. You want to test yourself.

Take the high-risk jobs, ones that no one knows anything about and that quickly provide an opportunity to learn. Surviving in such an entrepreneurial setting within an organization doesn't prove you can run a start-up company that's under funded and therefore has a lot more challenges.

It does indicate, though, that, if you're comfortable in that environment, you'll have a better chance of surviving on your own, where you have serious challenges without the support system of a larger or better financed company.

Another way to test your entrepreneurial IQ is to fantasize about running a company. When I worked for somebody else, I pretended the company was mine. If something went wrong, I took it as my responsibility. I always kept in mind the consequences of decisions I made that were affected by my superiors and those decisions that were mine alone. I'd ask myself: Would it have been a good decision or a bad one if I were in business for myself?

Often I found I was just as right as senior management. Although upper management's way prevailed, of course, I knew my decision also would have worked. By analyzing the outcome of my decisions while pretending the company employing me was mine, I gained confidence I could make the right decisions for a real company of my own.

Resist the urge to create a deadline or to set a time limit on your "apprenticeship." To set an arbitrary age by which you want to be running a business may not give you enough time to get the necessary experience or to go through the economic cycles of an industry you've chosen.

And if you have to start over training for a different business because the first one was the wrong fit, you'll either frustrate yourself by missing your deadline, or you'll cut short the training and jeopardize your chance of success. The training process takes as long as it takes. Enjoy it, with the objective in mind that, one day, you'll run a business and run it well.

Chapter 2
Acquiring a Business

I started my first real enterprise when I was about 16. It was 1955, and prosperity had arrived in the Midwest. Farmers had graduated to tractors and better farming equipment, leaving their old horse-drawn equipment to rust away among the trees and weeds.

Figuring they might like to get rid of all that old machinery, I started a hauling business with a friend who had a pickup. We called on farmers who had old machinery and abandoned cars lying around and offered to haul the junk away free – getting our pay at the junkyard in Norfolk, Nebraska.

The price of scrap metal wasn't much – about $50 a load. But even after we paid for gas, about 30 cents a gallon at the time, we could end up with more than $20 apiece for each trip.

From such ventures as this and from my job on the farm, I always had cash. In high school, I could even afford to hire schoolmates to type my papers. I came to appreciate early the freedom and independence discretionary income provided.

Looking for an Opportunity

Finding or starting a business usually isn't easy. You look for voids of unmet services in the community. You read the want ads. You study trade magazines for the industry that interests you. You check every nook and cranny. In fact, I suggest you pretend you're a newspaper reporter: Interview anyone who will talk to you. Ask about businesses like the one in which you're interested.

Still, you might not get it right the first time, or even the second.

Failure as Education

Many successful business owners have some failures in their history. What I learned from my failures has contributed greatly to my success.

With youthful optimism I quit a factory position. All the skills I had learned working on the farm, I thought, surely could get me a better job. I had been studying in a two-year program in construction technology, and I had a lot of home-construction equipment and tools from remodeling my home. So I did a marketing plan for a construction company and started Colony Construction with the money I had been saving.

Colony Construction was a one-man operation, and I soon discovered I couldn't make any money working solo in the construction business. Including the time spent estimating jobs and going to get materials, I couldn't recover my expenses and, at the same time, pay myself a decent hourly wage.

I was trying to make $20 an hour, and I was making only about 10 percent on my materials. If I bought a ton of block for a retaining wall and worked 10 hours on it, I'd earn $200 and have maybe only $100 markup on my materials. Plus, I had to absorb a lot of breakage and other costs. I also learned many people want a quality job but expect to pay a bargain price.

Next, a friend and I bought a decorative-plaster-plaque company, and I learned more. I had always liked art. I also enjoyed making things with my hands, and I knew how to build molds. I thought this would be a satisfying occupation for me.

We expanded our customer base and thought we were off to a good start, but we soon ran into trouble. Eventually, several problems conspired to drive us out of business, but the granddaddy of them all was that we didn't know anything about the industry. We bought the business because we could afford it and because we appreciated art.

Had we taken the time to learn about the industry, here's what we would have discovered:

At the time, several large companies already covered the plaster-plaque business quite well, companies too big and too established for us to compete against successfully.

Shipping plaster plaques across the country was difficult and could become prohibitively expensive because of breakage.

The industry has low start-up costs, which means it attracts too many people who run their business poorly and settle for a low profit margin. In a business that doesn't have a high capital investment, what you sell is labor, and it's difficult to make much money selling labor.

Our production was not likely to become a smooth operation. My partner and I had different ideas about how to make the plaques, including differing notions about what looked good. Although we worked probably 16 hours a day, we couldn't get ahead. Eventually, I tried to buy him out, but we couldn't come to terms. Then we tried to sell the business but failed at that, too. Finally, we closed. I lost a business, and I lost a friend.

The third business, a fast-food drive-through, wasn't a failure. In fact, I recently sold it. But I did make some mistakes that affected our success. One, I didn't evaluate the marketplace carefully enough. I thought there was a niche for a high-quality hamburger, because that's what I wanted. Ours were thick quarter-pounders patted by hand from fresh, never-frozen meat.

Instead, I found most fast-food eaters buy on price. And they certainly don't seek out "gourmet" burgers for their kids, who would rather have the plastic toys that accompany the meals sold by the national chains.

Two, I wasn't in the "loop" of fast-food business owners. Without networking, I didn't have enough information about good suppliers and service providers for the industry.

Three, when I started my burger shop, I was still running my steel-fabricating company. I didn't realize how much time and effort would be involved in making a real go of the burger business. It required more commitment than I could give it with all my other responsibilities and interests.

Be Diligent in Your Search

A common denominator in all three of these companies was my lack of relevant experience. The lesson is, and I cannot state it strongly enough: Whether you start a company or buy one, focus on an industry familiar to you. You'll have a better grounding for all the information you have to find out, such as how cyclical the business is, how long you think the lifetime of the company's product is, the inherent liabilities of the business, the competition, the maturity level of that business in relation to its marketplace. Ultimately, you're trying to figure the company's potential to create revenue and your ability to create profits from that revenue.

How can you determine whether a particular company offers a good opportunity for you? There's no single set of criteria. Each business has its own unique list, because each business differs from every other business, even within the same industry. And each company has skeletons in its closet, skeletons the owners don't want you looking at too closely.

You need good consultants to help you determine the company's true condition. Let me say specifically: You want advice from people who don't benefit from the sale of the company. You probably won't get usable advice from a business broker, who has a stake in selling you the company.

Rather, you need at least an accountant and an attorney. You want someone with an analytical mind, someone who can sort the data for the information you need. And you want an attorney who's experienced in corporate issues and contracts.

Industry experts would be helpful teammates. Look at the trade magazines for people who can provide insight. Look for academics with a background in the industry.

Talk to bankers for information about the local economy, the availability of credit, the potential financing issues.

Owners of other businesses like the one that interests you could provide useful information. When I was looking at the business I bought, I interviewed its customers and suppliers to find out why they dealt with the company. Would you prefer to hear "Because it's cheaper than anyplace else" or "Because the company is reliable"? Either answer provides a wealth of information.

Talk to administrators of the community in which the business is or will be located. They can tell you about local tax issues, zoning laws, restrictions on the business.

You need to ascertain the company's strengths and whether you can use them and enhance them. A cyclical business that's successful because the owner has been able to use his deep pockets and a good credit line to keep out competitors and fund downturns isn't the business for you if you don't have similar financial assets.

You want to ascertain a company's weaknesses and whether you can overcome them. Say you find a part-time business that makes lawnmowers, and the owner lays off the workers half the year. You might see the potential for a year-round business, because you can make snow blowers, too, with the same equipment and the same employees.

You want any information that pertains to the welfare of your future company. Do the employees have the right experience? Does the company have an adequate employee-retention record? Are key employees about to retire? Does the company have expensive apprenticeships associated with building the product or servicing clients? Is the pricing structure profitable enough?

You want to know why the company is on the market. Is the industry fading? Are liability issues too great to overcome at the company's current size? Is the owner tired?

Analyzing all the data, you alone must decide whether the business is a good opportunity for you. You alone know whether you have the requisite knowledge, experience, talent, and energy – and I want to emphasize energy – to succeed at it.

What a Business Is Worth

As badly as you might want to buy a particular business and as reasonable as you think the price is initially, you must consider your potential purchase with a realistic measure and with as much objectivity as you can muster. Here's the most important question to ask: "Is this business worth what the seller is asking for it?" You want to determine the potential of the business to generate revenue. And you want to assess your ability to manage that business well enough to generate sufficient profits from the revenue.

Let's say you're looking at a company with a selling owner who's tired and turning down a lot of work. It might be worth a higher asking price, because as a manager with energy and imagination, you know you immediately could generate more business.

When I was negotiating to buy my company, I put pencil to paper and saw I could make the numbers work with the owner's terms. I also saw he had enough projects from a single customer to pay his asking price; he didn't even need all the other accounts he had.

Evaluating a Business

There are three basic ways to evaluate the worth of a business. The most authentic uses a multiple of earnings. If the worth of a business that interests you is six times earnings, and the earnings are $100,000 a year, then the value of that business probably would be about $600,000. Small businesses generally are valued in the range of six to 10 times earnings. But a business in a growth industry, with the potential of increasing profitability to a higher percentage, might be valued at as much as 30 times earnings.

That's a broad range, because of the many factors specific to each business and to each industry. Even two similar businesses could be valued differently because of such variables as tenure of management, expertise of the current workforce, the extent of liability, or location.

A simple method of evaluating a business is to use an industry formula. For instance, the garbage pick-up industry says a business is worth so much per "container-yard." So a garbage-pick-up business is worth a multiple of that factor, depending upon the number of container-yards.

Another way to determine the worth of a business is to multiply book value by some factor. Book value is the value of a company's total assets, minus liabilities. It is an accounting term based on depreciated value, and it is not the same as market value. There are modifications of that formula; for instance, some evaluators use the replacement value of assets.

Intrinsic value can override book value. Let's say a company valued at two times book value owns a forest. If the stated book value doesn't take into account the dormant asset value of 2 trillion board feet of lumber that could be harvested from the forest, the actual asset value of the company is book value times a much higher multiple than the original multiple. That's a bargain for the astute investor.

Warren Buffett, chairman of Berkshire Hathaway, Inc., and one of the most successful investors of our time, found such a situation when he initially bought shares of Coca-Cola. He discovered that the company's book value did not include the intrinsic value of its instantly recognizable logo. Consequently, he determined that stock shares at the time of his purchase were at bargain prices.

This illustrates that the difference between book value and a higher current asset value is a gray area that may not be reflected in the selling price. No matter the income of a company, the unrealized value of the company's assets can provide a hefty economic advantage beyond the book value (and the selling price) of the company.

Of course, this is an overview. Evaluating a business usually is not an easy or a straightforward task. I'll say it again: You'll have a better idea of its actual worth if you stick with an industry familiar to you. Second stanza: Get an expert's opinion.

Forms of Ownership

I wouldn't presume to tell you how to own a business, because the possibilities vary with the situation. Laws at the federal, state, and local levels will affect your decision, as will your personal circumstances. So whether you are considering single ownership or a partnership, a closely held corporation, a public corporation, a limited liability corporation, employee ownership, or other possibilities, turn to your accountant and your attorney for advice.

Research the possibilities before you sign on the dotted line. One common and expensive mistake is to prepare the paperwork for one kind of enterprise then find you need a different kind. The required paperwork will be different, and you likely will have to reincorporate, restate the minutes, and refile the forms. In addition, a statute of limitations on when you can make changes might complicate the process. Know what the structure of your enterprise is going to be before you start the formal paperwork.

Partnerships

I had a partner in one business venture, and I wouldn't do it again. The success ratio of partnerships is no better than that of single-owner businesses and, in fact, may be worse because of the additional complications of ownership by more than one person.

In successful partnerships, the balance of power is stabilized to everyone's satisfaction. In reality, one person may be in charge, no matter what the paperwork says. Or the partners may have carved out their own responsibilities.

In one duo I know of, one partner was in charge of administration, the other of sales. Each thought his own department more important, so the two men left each other alone. They had a good working relationship, and they were a successful team.

Avoid the Devil in the Details

The company I own today came out of an asset purchase. That is, I didn't actually buy the company; I bought the machines and inventory, and I paid good will for the accounts. I didn't transfer existing stock; that process, in essence, transfers liability to the new owner. Instead, I issued new stock for my corporation. The name remained the same except for one detail: The original business was a company; mine is a corporation.

This way, I avoided all the liability of the previous owner's company.

This issue is especially important for a business that deals in capital goods, such as machinery. The original owner of my company had been building machines since 1946. I didn't want to assume his liability for machines I had no part in creating. Had I bought his company outright, rather than limit my purchase to the assets, I'd be the one sued if some worker got a hand caught in a machine built by the previous owner.

Why You Need a Contract

It might be romantic to imagine doing business the "old-fashioned" way – that is, sealing agreements with a handshake. Resist that temptation; it's too risky. You want documentation of your business transactions, even with family members. Circumstances change, memories fade, and should something happen to one of the parties, who else is going to know what they agreed to, so their wishes could be carried out?

Napkin Contract

I firmly believe where there are problems there are opportunities. An opportunity occurred for me during my employment with a steel company, where I learned about the metal-fabrication industry. Someone asked us to build a big wrought-iron fence. We were busy in the shop, but the man was a friend of the owners, so we agreed to do it.

The fence was a labor-intensive project. The architect had specified that it be made of square bar, with twists and points for the vertical members. We couldn't do the job right away, so I looked for a subcontractor. But wrought-iron fences are from a bygone era; nobody around could forge points on 5/8-inch-square, solid-steel bars.

At the same time, another guy, who bought steel from us and made machinery, asked me one day whether I could help him quote a job and buy steel for it. I told him about this fence project and asked if he could build a machine to make the pickets. Together, we designed a machine that used an abrasive grinder to point the bars and a hydraulic twister to twist them.

I got an agreement from my employers to do the subcontracting job myself, and we fabricated 15 tons of bars for that fence.

The steel company for which I worked frequently lost job bids, because certain processes were too difficult for the company to do economically or efficiently. With the fence project under my belt, I suggested setting up a subcontracting shop that could handle odd jobs. I would quote any project my employers couldn't do.

Now, everything I did during this time was with permission from my employers. It would have been unethical and unfair to go behind their backs. Besides, I valued their friendship and, of course, my job.

I was operating my subcontracting business from an old factory that had been flooded out and vacant for years. We had removed all the flood debris, repaired all the machinery, and gotten the factory running again. We had enough contracts to keep seven people working at night at that facility and to subcontract jobs to five other shops.

My men would show up at 6 p.m. and work until about midnight. I had an agreement with the owner of the facility to pay him $2.50 per man-hour that my people worked on my contract projects in his factory. The fee covered my use of the building, equipment, and electricity. If I had seven guys working six hours, I'd pay him for 42 hours; he would make $105 a night. I was paying about $750 a month.

After about a year, the owner demanded a monthly minimum of $2,000, although he hadn't made a dime on the factory in the previous 10 years. I thought his demand unreasonable and told him we'd be out in a week. The plant sat vacant until he died.

This change of events really pushed me. I looked for any business for sale. Finally, I got a call. One of my customers wanted to buy a steel-fabrication company and hire me to manage it.

The investment bankers handling the negotiations asked me to sit in as an adviser. I liked what I learned about the business, and I thought I could run it. But after weeks of effort, the negotiators had gotten nowhere. They had put all their energy into trying to convince the owner what he said he wanted wasn't what he really wanted. They finally gave up.

I asked to try to negotiate with him on my own behalf, and they agreed to let me have a go at it.

The owner and his attorney and I discussed the terms of the agreement. When it came down to the details, his request was so simple that spelling out the terms of the contract took only an hour. He wanted the purchase to be paid off in 10 years or less. He wanted a third of the sales price down. And he wanted X amount for the equipment.

I wanted a one-year "trial marriage" with the company. I wanted the right to refuse to buy the company if, at the end of that first year, I didn't want it. And I wanted half the year's profits if I did buy the company.

I wrote our terms up on a napkin at lunch. The owner's attorney drafted our agreement, and we made a deal. I still have the napkin.

Put Agreements in Writing

I absorbed an important lesson from my experience with the factory owner who raised the rent on me after I had cleaned up his flooded-out, vacant building and put his machinery to work again. The lesson was: Put agreements in writing. Had we had a contract, I wouldn't have been forced to make a decision between paying an exorbitant rent hike and finding another location for my company.

I remembered that lesson, and the contract I signed with the owner of the steel-fab company spelled out the terms of our agreement. Six months after our contract began, he tried to fire me. "You have so many jobs in the shop, I can't tell what's what," he said. In fact, at times the shop was full of my projects, a benefit to him as well. But he couldn't fire me: we had a contract.

Actually, he had sold his business four times before, but none of the other buyers had put anything in writing. Frustrated with all the new ideas these people had and all the projects they were doing, he ordered them to leave. Without a written contract, they had no choice.

I had a written contract. I stayed.

PART II

Now That You're In Business

Chapter 3
On Stewardship

O ne of the early, indelible lessons I learned on the farm was you couldn't slack off. In fact, for years after I left the farm, I had nightmares about forgetting to collect the eggs or milk the cows. We were responsible for our animals, which depended upon us.

Secondly, the farming community judged you by how well you cared for your livestock and your fields. A farmer who cut corners by overgrazing his fields or scrimping on fertilizer and not rotating his crops, so the soil could be restored, might ravage the land for a few years. Maybe he'd make a lot of money fast because he'd reduced his overhead, but he'd realize only a short-term gain.

About the third or fourth year, his yield would fall off, and if he hadn't cared for the soil, his farm would be worth much less than it had been when he started. Neighbors, who kept a watchful eye on each other's efforts and results, would have a lot to say about his practices.

Stewardship and patience for long-term results are deep-rooted values and for good reason: Success as a farmer hinges on them.

Stewardship and Success

Just as in farming, success in business flows directly from steward-ship. The issue isn't necessarily whether you can be profitable this year, but whether you can sustain your profitability with your current systems and practices. Put another way, planning for the short term or the long term will determine the strategies you apply and will indicate the quality of your stewardship.

Look Down the Road

Profitability in the short term does not guarantee profitability in the long term. A shortsighted "expert" can make changes that will improve the balance sheet in year one and destroy it by year five. For instance, he could eliminate all employees above a certain wage level. He could stop the research-and-development program and get rid of intermediate-term marketing programs, which of course means letting go the employees in those departments. He could even call for dropping some of the low-profit business and alienate customers by accepting only high-profit orders.

If this "expert" focuses just on month-to-month or quarter-to-quarter results, he might show good profits for a while, because he's reduced overhead. But such profits can't last. As many corporations that have downsized precipitously have realized too late, once you lose the ability to develop new products or programs, once you lose talented, experienced employees who are difficult to rehire or replace, the capacity to grow and remain profitable deteriorates.

I always have managed for moderate profitability, sustainable growth, and the ability to sustain employment for the people who work for me. A manager who has a short-term mentality is going to look like a hero following a manager like me. But, in turn, a farsighted manager following a guy like him is going to have a hard row to hoe, because he will have to redevelop the entire infrastructure, in the face of declining profits.

I also have managed with an eye toward long-term relationships with my employees, my vendors, my customers, my consultants. Continuity is important to me, for professional reasons as well as personal. A long-standing relationship with my accountants, for example, gives them the impetus to take continuing-education programs pertinent to my company's needs.

Building longstanding bridges between people helps sustain the company. When you do business with someone, keep in mind that bigger picture.

Succession Planning

A catastrophic event, such as death or a long-term illness, that affects a member of the management team presents a serious problem for an organization. But with succession planning, you put components in place to maintain your company's long-term viability if something like that happens.

You'll need financial resources to bridge the company's lost income, so consider key-person corporate insurance. It can cushion your losses, and it can help you underwrite the means of fulfilling the executive's responsibilities until that person returns to work or you find a replacement.

Filling the shoes of a missing executive won't be easy, but members of your staff might be capable of stepping into a management position or at least assuming some of the executive's duties, if you've planned ahead. Start at the hiring process by looking for applicants with the intelligence and ability to be trained for executive responsibilities. Then follow up with a cross-training program to increase the depth of management expertise.

A succession plan should include your consultants. Let's take an accountant, for instance. You could go bare bones on paying just for keeping the books and tax preparation. Or, better, you could educate your accountant with more details about your company and thus develop that person into a more useful resource. The extra fees you will pay for your accountant's time are good insurance for management continuity.

In an emergency, consultants might be able to help you by taking over some of the management tasks or by recommending someone, perhaps a retired executive, who could fill in. They'll be most helpful if you've kept them informed all along.

Carrying this thought one step further: When you hire consultants for a long-term project, look at the depth of their staff and the breadth of their professional connections. If something happens to the consultant with whom you're working, is someone available to quickly become familiar with your business and step in to complete the project?

Manage Risk

There are warranted risks. There are pointless risks. Consider what you would gain by doing something one way or another. Eliminate unnecessary risks. Even in everyday situations, consider the risk and decide if what you want to do is worth it.

For example, do you leave your car unlocked or, worse, leave the motor running while you run into the store for "just a moment"? Why do that? The chance that someone will steal your car may be small, but what possible gain is there in that situation that is worth the possible loss of your vehicle?

Cushion Risk with Cash

Because I make mistakes, I always try to fill the coffers before I head into a new risk venture. Accumulating cash before I launch helps cushion my calculated risks. I can play it safe, which I define as having considered all the risks and proceeding only when they have been minimized.

When the corporation and I were young, I took bigger risks than I do today. For one thing, I hadn't developed the responsibility toward my employees that I feel now. For another, my employees had not been with the company as long, and, had we failed, getting another job would have been easier for them then.

I'm more conservative now, and I feel an additional obligation because of the long tenure of many of my employees. And with so many more people riding this train with me, I feel even more strongly that I don't have the right to be a big risk taker with their cash and livelihoods. I take incremental risks now, rather than a big one all at once.

You Have a Lot to Lose

Philosophy or no philosophy, the ownership of anything, but especially brick and mortar – that is, buildings – tempers our behavior in ways that don't occur to those unencumbered by property. Ownership holds you in place and makes you accessible, accountable, and, especially, vulnerable. You are keenly aware that what you own and have worked so hard for can be damaged or taken from you.

Because of that concern, ownership, especially of brick and mortar, helps you become a better person. It forces you to behave more judiciously, more patiently, and with greater consideration for the consequences of your behavior. It gives you greater respect for the law. It forces you to exercise self-restraint. You even have to overlook some transgressions, because the possible ramifications of your response could be worse. You often have to turn the other cheek, as you remember that what you have to protect or lose is worth much more than "getting even" or destroying a relationship.

Company Culture

A workplace isn't a conglomeration of individuals; it's a community that functions much like a single entity. And, whether deliberately or inadvertently, top management greatly influences the culture of the workplace. The attitudes and values of those in charge of the workplace drive the focus, the "flavor," of the company.

Set High Standards

If management considers sales to be the starting point of all activity, the culture will be oriented toward rewarding salespeople strongly and treating the rest of the employees as support staff. On the other hand, leadership that emphasizes team effort is more likely to foster a culture of company-wide incentive programs and reward systems.

Management influences company culture not only through programs that are developed but also through people who are hired. At our company, we keep our group in mind when we hire, because teamwork is crucial. We want a cohesive and stable community of workers, so the group "fit" matters.

In fact, that quest for stability and continuity is one of the threads that bind our company culture. Another kind of company may need employees who work alone on separate projects. As such a business hires more and more people who like to work independently, its culture is more likely to evolve toward a structure that reinforces individuality rather than cohesiveness.

Management also molds and reinforces the company culture through policy – a code of standards, rules, even unwritten expectations. For example, federal laws set minimum standards, but I decided early I wanted more than just a minimally fit place of business; I wanted an outstanding one.

That value has guided us in all our decisions, including selecting employees, developing policies, instituting programs, and developing our marketing strategy.

We maintain a pleasant workplace, with art in the shop and a friendly cat named Numbers in the office area who visits with employees every day. Our culture seems to attract people who themselves have a higher standard. Those who don't appreciate the quality we emphasize weed themselves out.

One individual who comes to mind is the employee who wore a dirty T-shirt with vulgar words on it when we hosted an event for some guests in the shop. He had to be told to cover the shirt. With the kind of mentality that would guide him to wear a low-class piece of clothing to work, he belonged at a place with standards as low as his: someplace with filthy floors, dingy walls, and bad air-exchange. He didn't stay long.

We try to examine every aspect of our work community for ways to improve it, and we deal immediately with anything that detracts from the quality to which we aspire. If I find graffiti on the door of a toilet stall, for instance, we talk about it, and we clean it up right away. We don't tolerate even little acts of vandalism, because one small act of disrespect leads to another. And we have little of that.

Cleaning up after oneself rather than leaving a mess for somebody else to attend to, practicing good hygiene – those are basic expectations. But, though people generally know how to behave around others, some occasionally need to be reminded. A few even need to learn for the first time. The guy I saw spit on the floor prompted me to set a formal rule: Don't spit on the floor.

Taking good care of the work environment sends the message: I care about my employees and I have high standards. I am a good steward of this business, and I expect my employees to be good stewards of the company that provides them a livelihood.

Our policies emphasize stewardship, and I ask all the leaders in my company to emphasize it. I like to think that, in some ways, our company culture raises the expectations and elevates and maintains the standards for all of us.

Responsibility to Employees

Pettiness, meanness, silliness are all aspects of human nature that occasionally bedevil the best of us. And let's face it: even a saint, maybe especially a saint, can get on our nerves. But as an employer, you have answered a higher calling. You have assumed responsibility for the welfare of all your employees, and that includes their families.

It's an awesome burden, one under which you cannot behave frivolously or cavalierly. For that reason, you must control your urges to retaliate against employees who occasionally throw their emotional curve balls at you. The mandate that guides me in managing employees, and here I pass it on to you, is: To the best of your ability, be firm, fair, and consistent.

Make your decisions based on facts, not emotion, and be prepared to stick with them.

If you do something for one employee, treat his peers the same way. Realize that, even if you are a revolutionary, someone who likes to make sweeping changes, many of the people working for you are evolutionary at most. And some may not want their situation to change even one iota. Accommodate your employees' need for security by involving them in decisions, by putting your ideas into effect in measured steps, and by trying to be consistent. If you are erratic or impulsive, you will frighten employees, who can't possibly see from your perspective.

Establishing traditions can provide comfort. We have steak fries for outstanding monthly sales. We also have an annual Christmas dinner, awards for anniversaries of employment, and a monthly newsletter. By maintaining continuity, a string of celebrated events between the present and the past helps alleviate the fear of the unknown that so frequently accompanies change.

Reinforcing Community

There are businesses where employees play rotten tricks on each other for "fun." We have seen to it that our corporate community, instead, is a group in which people can trust each other. One employee who had been with us about a year said to the foreman, "You know, this is the best place I've ever worked. You don't need to be looking behind you all the time. Nobody's trying to stab you in the back around here." I don't know if he meant that literally or figuratively.

We reinforce our community cohesion in many ways. We use a single lunchroom for all employees; there's no private executive suite. We recognize people's special days, if they don't mind that kind of publicity – birthdays, wedding announcements, anniversaries, the birth of children, years with the company, and so forth. And, of course, the traditional events and projects help keep us together.

Other Important Corporate Values

In addition to stewardship, quality, and community, other values are worth mentioning: respect, for example. One of the simplest ways to express respect is to use good manners. Saying "please" and "thank you," holding the door for someone, letting the other person go first, being considerate of another's feelings and beliefs, listening without interrupting, all are part of the Golden Rule (Do unto others as you would have them do unto you).

Wearing appropriate clothes for your audience is another simple way to show respect. If you're going to meet with a suit-wearing, briefcase-toting group, accommodate their view of the world by dressing to meet their expectations.

If you're talking with someone whose vocabulary isn't as big as yours, lower your syllable count a notch. The whole point, presumably, is not to impress that person with your smarts, but to communicate so you can be understood. Showing off will only make the person resent you. What have you gained besides an enemy?

For that matter, you also can add to your list of enemies by talking down to people, including employees. Nobody likes being patronized.

Compassion is another important value. It is worth remembering that occasionally each of us goes through difficult times. When an employee has a problem, show that person some concern.

In fact, a corporate leader ought to run every decision through a filter of empathy. Running a company, you'll always have problems to solve. You'll always have someone asking for something. Rather than look at a request or a decision only in terms of what it can do for your bottom line, consider it also from an empathetic or a humane point of view: Is this a good thing to do? Is this the right thing to do?

No matter how much the legal profession may indicate to the contrary, a corporation is not merely an impersonal entity. It is you and your employees who give your corporation a heart.

Mind you, a compassionate business culture needn't be indulgent. Letting a habitually late employee off the hook because he can give you a heartrending excuse each time makes you credulous rather than compassionate. Moreover, it hurts the morale of the other employees who make the effort to be on time.

The rights of the individual are important, but community values take precedence in the workplace. There is no room for prima donnas. Every time I hire somebody, promote somebody, or terminate somebody, I'm trying to add value to my corporate community. I want to have a great work community so every employee has a good and productive work situation and the corporation is rewarded economically. Then, the corporation, in turn, can reward its employees.

Our first responsibility – the one I take the most seriously – is to our employees. But the larger community also has a place among our considerations, and so I want to mention altruism as a corporate value. Altruism is more than giving; it's giving without any expectation of return.

But let's face it: In most cases, corporate giving isn't altruism. Corporations often donate for the publicity it will bring them or to

curry favor with someone. Company-sponsored games, races, and per-
formances are good examples. Fair enough. But there are many opportunities around you for real corporate altruism. Be careful about your
choices, though, because your company also represents your employees. They might resent the company's supporting a group they dislike.

A company can contribute to worthy causes, but you don't necessarily have to make a cash gift. You can give in lots of ways, such as in-
kind gifts, in which you donate services or items, instead. Or you
might give time, serving on boards in the community or volunteering
the time of your employees to help on a project.

Even being a community activist who brings about needed changes
can be an altruistic venture. You might spend hours and effort convincing the county surveyor and other government officials they should
allocate the funds for a bridge over a dangerous set of railroad tracks.
You will help save lives, the ultimate in altruism.

Dealing with Government Agencies

Speaking of good relationships, I cannot overemphasize the importance of a cooperative attitude toward government agencies. When I
bought the company, many things about it were not up to standards.
The machinery was in bad shape, but I knew I could fix it. The building itself, which I didn't own, also was in bad condition.

The Occupational Safety and Health Administration (OSHA) was
just a couple of years old, but it carried a big stick. A compliance officer could drop in on a company unannounced and inspect the premises. Violations were grounds for a fine. Policies haven't changed much.

I knew I couldn't use a building that was not in compliance, and I
knew getting inspected was just a matter of time. So I paid for an
expert's survey of our deficiencies, then secured an application for a
hardship loan from the Small Business Administration (SBA) to bring
the building and equipment into compliance myself. The SBA then
would give the information to OSHA, from which point I would have
a grace period for completing the necessary repairs, a time during
which OSHA could not spring a compliance inspection on me.

Paranoia and premonition are blood brothers. I had a feeling that,
probably sooner rather than later, we were going to get a visit from an

OSHA random-investigation officer. I wasn't taking any chances. I wanted to be ready. I told my accountants to do an annual report three months ahead of time. I got the paperwork from the accountants for my application. I had all the materials in a box, waiting for an appointment, but the officer at the local SBA office couldn't see me for five days.

I was one day away from presenting my paperwork to the SBA when an OSHA inspector walked through the door. By law, he was not supposed to leave the premises once he had announced himself as a compliance officer. But I told the officer about all I had done – the new business I had just bought with all its deficiencies, the $5,000 study I had commissioned, the loan application to the SBA ready for the appointment for which I was waiting – all to prove I was in the process of complying, not avoiding.

He called his office and explained my circumstances. His supervisor told him to leave the premises. I think that was as gracious a gesture as any government representative could make. So I have no complaints about how I've been treated by OSHA, compared with the stories I've heard from some people.

I have found that an attitude of cooperation goes far in dealing with government agencies. Better to indicate you want to comply properly and to treat agency officials as if they were partners in the effort than to create an adversarial relationship with them. I have to believe that, for the most part, laws were enacted with the right motives, if not always the soundest reasoning.

At our company, we believe strongly in not violating law – any law – in the operation of our business. We have even written that intent into our corporate mission statement.

Ask for Ideas

Democracies don't work in the business environment. Ultimately, somebody has to be in charge. That's me in my company, you in yours. But just because the buck stops at my desk and yours doesn't mean we are free to make unilateral decisions, not, that is, if we want to avoid jeopardizing morale.

If I come up with a concept about how to do something, I don't say "Do it" just because I'm the boss. I involve my employees in decisions that affect them. That's one of the easiest and best ways to gain their support and their cooperation. And it lets them know I think they have worthwhile ideas to contribute. I owe them that.

Don't be like the owner who ordered a $100,000 piece of equipment before talking to his people in the shop. (It wasn't me.) When this machine arrived on the dock, can you imagine how they felt?

They should have participated in the decision to buy it, because any machine is going to be made useful by the employees who operate it. I certainly would want them in my corner when the time came to train on the machine, to run it, and to do preventive maintenance, because I'm not going to be looking over their shoulders to supervise them when they're working with it.

Set Up for Input

You have to condition subordinates to know you truly want their honest opinion. You have to phrase questions so you don't create a bias, so you aren't just fishing for confirmation of your own ideas. You want a real dialogue about options. If you have laid the proper groundwork, your employees won't be simply "'Yes' men."

I study the options, and I let the employees study the options. Then I might ask the maintenance person, "What do you think about machines A, B, and C? Which one will be the easiest to maintain?" "I like machine A," he might say. "Lubrication of the blades is easy, and the computer components are solid-state." Then to the person who's going to run the machine: "What do you think about this machine?" "Well," he might say, "the switch is too high, so it's unhandy. And there's no light fixture here." I get feedback that confirms what I already thought or gives me more information to consider.

Then I create a matrix that indicates each participant's rating of the machines, and I factor out the best option. I don't just tell my employees to pick a machine; I create a process that picks the machine. Ultimately, the decision and the final responsibility are mine, but I've paid my employees the respect of requesting their involvement.

Besides, I'm the first to admit I need their help; one person can't know everything.

I enlist the advice of others in helping me make a decision, but if it doesn't work, the failure is mine. Perhaps I haven't involved the right people or asked the right questions or followed up on incomplete advice. But I can't blame anyone else, because no one else has as complete a picture as I do.

Keep Information Flowing

Businesses never become perpetual-motion machines. They require constant tinkering. Even a lemonade stand needs tinkering, or managing, as it's usually called. A manager is always looking for what's going wrong, plugging holes in the dike, so to speak. You have to listen, take in information, put order to what you learn, and make an action plan.

The process isn't complicated, but often it's difficult, because running a company is a little like the old "piñata" party game. You're the kid in the blindfold, and you're depending on everyone around you for information that will guide you to the piñata, so you can whack it open and everyone can get the goodies inside. Except that the business version of the game has a twist to it: Your employees don't always feel comfortable telling you what you need to know, particularly if you don't ask.

Why don't they? One answer is obvious: sometimes they're afraid. They're afraid they will lose status, respect, their job, their security. Certainly, if you throw a tantrum when someone tells you something unpleasant, word will get around quickly that you are prone to shooting the messenger.

As an owner or a manager, far from being at the center of your work community, you actually are at the edge of it. The power of your authority creates a moat around you, and the only bridge across it to your employees is your constant effort to keep communication open—especially, to make it easier for them to tell you the truth and the whole truth, as they see it.

Still, the process of getting information is seldom straightforward. No one is going to come up and blurt out what's going on. You have to look for clues – body language, side comments, hints that there is more than meets the eye. Of course, positive information flows much more freely than negative. But negative reports are more important; they are the guides to the problems that undermine your success.

It is up to you to create an environment comfortable enough that the truth will emerge, like a turtle that peaks its head out of its shell and resumes crawling once it senses it won't be harmed. Concentrate on diminishing the feeling of jeopardy employees may have when they give you negative information. Try to avoid putting them on the spot.

Talk about problems in terms of improving the company as a whole. Ask questions in an objective format. For example: What could make this workplace better for you? How could we make this task easier? What could we do to keep this mistake from happening again? Above all, never ask employees for negative information about their fellow workers.

Successful businesses are those that make mistakes, then rebound and grow beyond them. So make your workplace one in which employees can readily admit their mistakes, then work on a solution. It is up to you whether your employees become better at what you want them to do or better at hiding their mistakes.

This isn't to say you must tolerate repetition of the same errors. We once had an employee who let his wife call him frequently at work. Her phone calls distracted him so much that he lost focus and made mistakes. We told him to quit taking her calls at work, so he sneaked them at lunch. But it didn't matter that she called him on his lunch break; he still got upset. He wouldn't take control of his situation and fix his problem, so he continued to make preventable mistakes. After he cost us thousands of dollars, we had to let him go.

Loyalty: The Best Consistency

One of the great disillusionments an employer suffers is the realization that employees don't share the employer's dream. But how could they? The janitor can't appreciate the company from the owner's perspective. The owner's fantasy is fueled by a belief in the probability of his own success. His sureness comes from "knowing" that he's capable of making the dream a reality. And ownership of that dream supplies his determination and fortitude.

On the other hand, employees come by the belief in the employer's dream secondhand. In the hiring process, the dreamer, you, convinces them of your ability to bring their fantasy to fruition. They choose to join you in the venture, but they never fully own it like you do.

Instead, consider what employees *can* offer: loyalty. As keeper of the fantasy, you can reinforce their loyalty by paying competitive wages and benefits. You can do it by creating a less stressful environment, one in which a certain amount of fulfillment exists. You can do it by maintaining fulltime employment and, thus, their job security.

And you can do it by sharing with them the gradual realization of the dream, the profits. Our annualized rate of turnover for fulltime employees for the past 30 years has averaged eight percent, largely, I believe, because of these efforts.

There is a tradeoff between salary and job security. High salaries that cannot be sustained in a down market mean employment volatility, and fast growth that compromises the future of a company jeopardizes the financial stability of workers and their families.

Instead, I have chosen to grow our company at a pace that we can maintain from year to year, so that we can support our entire work force through varying economic conditions. That's how I express my loyalty to my employees.

Our conservative approach has enabled us to keep our work force intact for more than 30 years, even through a serious economic downturn. In 1981, the country was in the worst recession I've seen since I bought the company. Orders had slacked off. In fact, our customers were laying off workers. So were many of our competitors. And I lost $365,000 that year.

But of my 20 employees then, I didn't lay off a single one. Instead, I made jobs for those who didn't have a project on which to work. They painted. They expanded the shop. They put siding on the building. They upgraded equipment. They conducted training programs. They geared up for the end of the recession, whenever that might occur.

By providing continuity of employment, I gave them my loyalty; but I also had practical reasons for keeping all of them. The training I gave them was expensive. I couldn't easily replace them because they had learned many of their skills on the job, not in school.

Additionally, I knew, when the recession ended, our customers would have a tremendous pent-up need. By keeping my work force intact, we were ready for the opportunities that came our way. We all benefited.

Loyalty is an important element of success, and it's a two-way street. At the same time, I realize many Generation X-ers have reason not to be loyal; experiences they have had in the marketplace haven't necessarily rewarded loyalty. But there are companies, such as ours, that do deserve loyalty. In fact, we consider it our obligation to give our employees a work environment that fosters loyalty.

Communication

The hefty word "communication" comprises 13 letters, divisible into five syllables. This hulk of a word carries so much meaning that millions of other words have been written and spoken about it, and still there is no end in sight to our quest for understanding, especially of its importance in business. I offer here a few simple observations.

To Say the Least

I like to talk. Most people like to talk. And we practice a lot, so talking is easy. It's listening that's hard. That end of the conversation is work, work, work. Occasionally, I play a little personal game to practice listening. I call it a "contest to say the least." In this contest, I try to let the other person talk as much as possible. I respond only in ways that encourage elaboration.

Now, there is active listening and there is passive listening. I would call my contest active listening, when I am trying to understand the other person's point of view by asking pertinent questions or making reflective comments. And I think we have an obligation as a participant in any conversation to be an active listener, to ask questions if we aren't following what someone is telling us.

Passive listening, on the other hand, occurs when we simply are waiting for a turn to speak or when we are quiet only because we aren't paying attention or don't have anything to say. Passive listening doesn't further real communication; active listening does.

In real dialogue, there's a time to listen and a time to talk, generally. The process is an exchange in which you're part of the conversation, interacting with the other person or other people. And if dialogue is the intent, you have to share both the floor and the effort.

Where Confusion Reigns

Two people in conversation don't have to be speaking different languages to misunderstand one another. Especially for important issues, I cannot stress enough that you verify that the other person heard you correctly. The same goes for you: Confirm that you understood what the other person was trying to get across to you.

Pilots and air-traffic controllers do this as a matter of safety. When you're flying an airplane in the traffic pattern over a congested airport, hearing and understanding instructions correctly could be a matter of life and death.

In daily life, as well, although the situation might not cause wake turbulence or a near miss, as in flying, getting what you want depends upon clarification. None of us sees life and its situations exactly as another person does.

A little episode I recently had illustrates that point. I asked my wife to pick up some cough drops for me on her next trip to the store. I had been taking a Robitussin drop for a while, but I switched to Hall's. I went so far as to tape a Hall's wrapper to the grocery list, but my wife brought home the Robitussin drops.

In our ensuing conversation, I discovered that she thought I was just using the Hall's wrapper as a generic reminder to get me cough drops. Now, how is it that two people who communicate intimately and daily can misunderstand one another on such a simple issue? Once I realized she was thinking in general terms, while I was being specific, I understood. It would have helped had I verified the message.

How much more difficult it is for people in less personal business environments to interpret one another's messages correctly. I reiterate: On important issues, ask a question at least two different ways, so you can uncover possible traps of detail.

Be especially careful using words open to subjective interpretation. What do you mean when you say "quality," for example? Do you think your listener has the same understanding? I learned that lesson the hard way, with a customer who ordered a machine built with "regular" stainless steel. His idea of "regular" was as polished as a chrome sink backsplash he'd seen. Mine, on the other hand, was a 2-B finish, which is how stainless steel arrives from the mill.

I built the machine according to my notion of "regular." And my customer was dismayed when he saw the product. Had we clarified what we meant by "regular" with actual samples or a comparison to something both of us could reference, we would have avoided frustration, unnecessary expense, and hard feelings.

Confusion occurs, too, when you let stand an incorrect statement. I don't mean you have to go around correcting every misstatement you hear. I am speaking of remarks pertaining to your business. As a company leader, you have a responsibility to correct such misstatements, especially those made by employees.

If you don't correct the person, you are confirming to the individual that he is, in fact, correct, and you are letting him function under a wrong belief. In some instances, such misunderstandings cause tremendous and expensive trouble. Verify and, when necessary, correct – politely, of course.

A Telling Image

The clothes we wear carry messages for us, and we can use that fact to bridge the little social gaps that exist between us and others. There are those for whom personal image is tantamount to an art form. But in business, when we are trying to connect with others who can help us, self-expression is not the issue; communication is.

A suit may not be an important part of your wardrobe, but if you're going to meet with people who wear suits, don't dress in your usual sweatshirt and jeans; wear a suit that day. The group will know that you have at least some little thing in common and, in such a situation, the twain are more likely to meet.

You see, difference begets caution, caution leads to reserve, and reserve makes openness to the ideas of others that much more difficult.

So the fewer the differences between you and your audience, the better your chances of persuasion, collaboration, negotiation, and success. When your image seriously differentiates you, you have more to overcome to get others to accept and trust you. Do you do business with people you don't trust?

You want as little as possible to interfere with your message. So if you think your image will detract from your communication with someone, the solution is simple: Alter your image so you fit the likely expectations of that person.

A young acquaintance of mine, who raises funds for an art-residency program, commented on the reception she had gotten from some business people who were potential donors. She had decided to wear a suit to the meeting rather than her usual creative attire. She expressed relief at her decision, noting that the group accepted her immediately and took seriously what she had to say. This isn't deception; it's showing respect for your audience and presenting your best self.

Pathologies of Information

To make the most of information, apply a healthy skepticism and an awareness of the context in which the message is given. A skeptic recognizes, at some level of awareness, that information is not pure. That is, it is not totally true, nor is it necessarily totally false. In fact, we probably have a skeptic to thank for outlining the ways in which information is distorted, however unintentionally.

Most of us know that information indeed is distorted; it's never absolutely true. But we're looking for what's mostly true, and we're looking for whether the important parts of the message are true. Describing some of the "pathologies" of information serves to illustrate how it can be tainted and what we should consider when we read or hear something.

First of all, there is pure and simple ignorance. That is, the source of information doesn't know what he's talking about.

Next, in terms of culpability, is bias. In this case, the person providing the information has a vested interest in making sure you think the way he wants you to think.

For instance, let's say you walk into a shoe store where the salesperson gets a 15-percent commission for selling the pink shoes and a 10-percent commission for selling the black ones. Which shoes do you think that salesperson is going to push? Those pink shoes wear well. They look great on you. They're easy to maintain and they go with just about everything. It isn't that the black shoes wouldn't wear just as well, look just as good, and go with just as many clothes.

But the salesperson doesn't tell you that; he has a vested interest in trying to get you to buy those pink shoes. Now, if you aren't aware of that commission lurking in the background, you won't know about the salesperson's bias, and you might be inclined to accept at face value what he says and not think any further. Perhaps you'd have liked the black shoes better.

Of course, bias can be inadvertent, too. We do tend to see what we want to see. Education, background, and experience all shape our point of view. People who try to achieve objectivity, journalists, for example, try to ferret out their own bias as well as that of others. But, in fact, objectivity exists only as an ideal.

Another pathology is "finagled" information. A source is vague or misleading, omits important details, or lets a mistaken assumption stand.

For example, someone has a pen you like, and you say, "Boy, that's a beautiful pen; I'll bet that's solid gold." The person knows it's only plated gold but doesn't tell you. "I'd really like to have that pen," you say. "Would you sell it to me?"

The owner says, "Oh, no. A friend gave me this pen. It's priceless to me." You say, "Would you consider selling it for $1,000?"

The owner-turning-seller replies, "Well, if you want it that badly, I'll sell it to you for $1,000." You buy the pen.

Later, you discover that it's gold-plated, not solid gold. You try to return the pen. "Look," the person says, "I didn't even want to sell the pen. I didn't say it was solid gold; you did. I don't have an obligation to correct what you think you know. You came to your own conclusion, and you bought the pen."

He hasn't lied to you outright, perhaps, but he's limited the truth by not correcting your wrong assumption. Whose responsibility is that?

Such misinformation is common, and the court dockets are full of law-suits trying to answer that very question.

Fraud obviously is the most damaging kind of misinformation. Fraud is total misrepresentation, even lying. Serious enough and it's a crime.

The skeptic doesn't trust anything at face value, nor does he dismiss information out of hand. The skeptic protects his interests by question-ing the information source thoroughly and by trying to discern what the source's biases might be. He also checks other sources for a second or even third opinion. And if he makes assumptions, he verifies them.

Checks and Balances

Don't trust even your mother. As wonderful a person as she is, she can't do everything well. No matter how close to perfection we are, we need someone to check our work, because we all forget sometimes, we all mess up. Even bosses need someone to check their work.

Above all, don't assume you can hire someone to do a job and not monitor that person's work. Nor should you ever take for granted something will be done correctly. You are safer assuming it won't, so a big mistake doesn't catch you off guard.

I don't mean you should oversee every single detail. You can't do that if you're running the show. But you can build checks and balances into your system that provide oversight without creating an oppressive environment.

Set Up Processes

Businesses can fail because little things fall through the cracks. Incoming checks get lost. Supplies disappear. Mortgage payments don't get made. Important financial deadlines slide by. As your company grows, more things are prone to falling through the cracks, unless you create a system to account for them.

For example, at our company, we can compare a tentative bill of materials for a job with what our records show we actually used, because we have computerized our inventory list. We keep a list of pro-jects, big and small, that have been assigned to people, and I check off the projects as they're completed. In fact, the whole company is a system of checks and balances.

Consider what information you need and create as simple a system as you can. Many times, you can protect yourself by requiring that a journal be kept or a report be done on a certain schedule.

Let's say you perform a service for clients on an appointment basis. You need to know how much business you do each day, how much you collect, and how much is owed you. Perhaps a simple ledger with three columns – cash, credit, and accounts receivable – reviewed daily at close of business would be sufficient.

Above all, keep up with your records. The sooner you write down the necessary information, the better you'll remember the situation you're monitoring.

Foil Sticky Fingers

We don't want to think people we hire can't be trusted, but the sad fact is some among us can't resist easy temptation. You continuously have to assess your vulnerability in every operation of your company. Look for ways to limit opportunities for the crook. Especially, consider how employees prone to "sticky fingers" can take advantage of you.

Anything is subject to theft. We once caught an employee stealing soap, for crying out loud. Keep supplies under lock and key, and don't put them by an exit door.

When you let people handle checks and cash, systems of checks and balances are essential. I segregate checks immediately by putting them into a clear vinyl arranger. They go to a certain spot on my desk.

When I give a check to the person who makes out the deposit slip, I write the amount of the check and the date I received it on the envelope in which the check arrived, and I slip the envelope into the top right drawer of my desk.

When the deposit has been made, I initial the deposit slip, to indicate I've seen it. Only then do I throw away the envelope. If an envelope is in the drawer, I know I have to follow up on something.

One of my habits is to look at the ledger of receipts every day and to check the age of the accounts receivable.

These simple acts have many benefits. I get a sense of where the money's coming from and whether customers are paying on a timely basis. I can check up on new customers: credit, history, size, the chance of doing business with them again, and so forth. I can praise a salesperson for doing a good job: "That looks like a nice account. Keep up the good work."

If you check all your cash receipts and charges at the end of the day and deposit daily all your checks along with your cash, you leave a smaller window of opportunity for the employee who might be looking for extra cash to buy a new car or pay off a gambling debt. As a backup policy, use an outside auditor or bookkeeper to balance your books monthly, even if you have a bookkeeper on staff.

Use a Time Clock

Many employees on the time clock at our company would be salaried workers at other companies. We manage our payroll this way because it is an honest program that is fair to the employee and fair to the company. Fewer opportunities exist for the employee or the company to take advantage of the other.

Let's consider the discussion of salary in a job interview. The interviewer says that the job pays $400 a week.

An unscrupulous potential employee might do this version of fancy math in his head: I'll agree to work 40 hours for $400 a week, but if I average only 38 hours a week, I actually will make more than $10 an hour. (If he's really quick, he'll know that it's a pay increase of more than 5 percent.)

At the same time, an unscrupulous supervisor might think: This person agrees to work 40 hours for $400 a week. But, if I tell him he's going to have to work a little extra during the busy season, maybe I can get him to average 42 hours a week. Then I'll really be paying him less than $10 an hour ($9.52 to be exact).

Right off the bat, a pattern of taking advantage of the other party begins, and it will continue to poison the relationship between employer and employee.

Using a time clock protects both parties. If the employee works 42 hours, he gets two hours of overtime pay; if he works 38 hours, the employer subtracts two hours' pay from his weekly check. And if you need a worker to do a special job on overtime, more than likely he will do it.

Even a time-clock system isn't trouble free. Overtime is a quick way for employees to give themselves a raise. How do you keep them from wasting time during the day or dragging out their work into overtime? You supervise them.

Outside the Company

Corporations, no matter what size, are not islands unto themselves. They exist within a community, and they rely on the business environment their community provides them. Altruism aside, it behooves corporations to show appreciation for that environment.

The results of "an attitude of gratitude" are multiple. Certainly, the generosity of a company to its community will be repaid with better public relations. Even if the charitableness doesn't directly generate more business, it will help combat the anti-business sentiment that permeates public consciousness. People look favorably on a company that contributes to its community.

Who is your community? You have to decide that for yourself. It depends upon which group provides customers, but also employees and, perhaps, even vendors. We can interpret the concept of community as neighborhood, city, county, state, region, country, even world. Certainly, special-interest groups can constitute a community.

Get Involved

The point is: Get involved in something bigger than your company. For example, we have given time to the University of Nebraska by supporting programs and by providing knowledgeable employees to serve on committees that address issues related to our industry.

Another important way to contribute is to get involved in legislation that affects your business. Become politically active. We contribute at the state and national levels by supporting candidates who are pro-business, candidates who endorse bills that are in the interest of business, such as those that improve product-liability laws. These contributions indirectly support the company, which provides the jobs that give my employees the ability to make a better living.

Join trade organizations that pertain to your industry. For instance, the most general one here is the Nebraska Chamber of Commerce and Industry. Belonging to it provides a good education. We get to exchange information about all kinds of concerns: suppliers, employee problems, political issues. And members can have greater legislative influence as part of a group than as individuals.

Join boards that make policy. Concerned citizens are generous to give their time to community boards, but many members have little understanding of how their decisions affect businesses. They need the perspective and advice you can provide as a businessperson. Join service clubs or business groups that share your interests. Support community projects. Engage in public speaking.

A cynic might view these efforts as mere enlightened self-interest. No matter. It is a bigger-minded self-interest, with further-reaching consequences that positively affect others, than merely looking out for Number One.

Networking

A gathering of cows at the water trough looks like a coffee klatch. One can imagine the bonny bovines comparing notes on who found the best grass that day, or whether anybody noticed the weak spot in the west fence line that could be gotten through without too much effort, or who agrees that the new farmhand's milking technique needs a little work. In business, if you don't gather with others occasionally to talk and listen, you're going to miss out on important and useful information.

I cannot overstate the importance of networking. One reason my burger business, a sideline interest, wasn't sufficiently successful was I didn't network effectively. I was out of the loop of that industry, so I didn't have enough current information about the local market. If you don't know how much a fry cook gets paid in your area, how can you hire effectively? I should have networked in that industry before I started the business.

Networking doesn't have to be a formal process; in fact, more often it is not. Having lunch with someone, playing golf, getting involved in community projects, serving on boards — all are good ways to get into the circuit of ideas.

The important thing is to find out what's going on around you and, in a new industry, to learn enough to make the decision to enter it before you become an insider. The scuttlebutt you hear might help you avoid becoming one of the victims of a customer's bankruptcy. You might hear about a good potential employee. You might discover some new markets.

Protect Your Golden Goose

Your business provides you with the means to support yourself and your family. You know your public life affects the well being of your business. But have you also considered the effect your private life has on it? You see, a business owner is never really "off duty." Everything you do and stand for reflects on your business.

Remember that, because you want to enlist the support of the community whenever you can. You want people on your side. You want them to say, "I would rather help this guy than his competitor."

What does your home look like, and what message do you think it gives the public about you? It should look like you are the owner, or the manager, of a company. Your image even extends to your car. It may not be the newest model, but it should be clean inside and outside and ready for taking a customer or an employee someplace.

You want to convey an image of success, but also keep in mind your employees' point of view. The employee or customer who sees you driving the most expensive car might resent you for your immoderate taste, compared with what he can afford.

What does your personal appearance indicate? Do you project an aura of responsibility? I cannot state this clearly enough: Your appearance is important. The question to ask yourself is: How should I look for my station in life? You get more respect from people if you look the role.

Consider whether your activities and hobbies convey an image of respectability and whether your actions as a citizen indicate concern for your community. You get business and support from it. Do you give your share of time and effort to community projects or boards? Are your relationships with your employees, vendors, customers, and community good and fair?

The quality of your life, private as well as public, does affect your business. Protect it by always conducting yourself properly.

Manage Your Life

Managing your business is really about managing your life. That is, it is just an extension of your life; it is not a separate entity. Managing your business, your life, anything, stems from values, practical as well as moral, that are part of your philosophy. They should provide the rationale, the basis, for your decisions.

If you believe lying and cheating are wrong, you will decide against shortchanging customers. If you believe quality is important, you will opt for the best components to put into your products. If you think people should be treated with respect, you will develop personnel policies reflecting that belief.

But your values, and your philosophy, help you only if you pay attention to them. You can't put them on the back shelves of your mind, to be brought out and leafed through only for academic discussions.

Get a Hobby

One of the problems of a growing new business, especially for a person inexperienced in business who is trying to put things in perspective, is that the business becomes his hobby, too. In fact, it becomes his life. So I strongly suggest: Get a real hobby. It's one of the healthiest things you can do for yourself and for your business.

I don't mean fishing and hunting once a year or going on vacation. I mean getting outside your company into an environment where you are not in charge. Find something different from what you do all day. Take some classes. Learn to play a musical instrument. Maybe you'd like to do something altruistic, such as serving on community boards.

Just get into a situation where you are not under pressure for the outcome, where the only one to whom you are responsible is yourself. You need the mental break. What's more, the rejuvenation and the flow of new ideas you gain from putting yourself into new and different environments can give you a fresh perspective on work issues. In the long run, your company will benefit from your mental change of pace.

Draw the Line Between Business and Friendship

It's always tempting to cut some slack for a friend. Just remember, any discount you give a friend that you wouldn't ordinarily give another customer is a gift. Ask yourself, how big a gift would I give this person in a normal social environment?

A discount amounting to hundreds of dollars may be an unwittingly generous act, if for special occasions you normally give that person a card and a bottle of wine.

Chapter 4
Planning, Research, and Decision Making

In the shortages during and after World War II, most farmers repaired a broken part or modified something else to fit; they didn't buy a new one. It took a lot of thinking, and it was a lot more challenging than just driving up and down the field on a tractor.

As a boy on the farm, I liked working on equipment. I liked figuring out what was wrong, then figuring out how to fix it. We had to know what was needed, what to keep in stock in the shop, how to remove usable parts from unused equipment to repair what was broken, what kinds of tools we needed for repairs, how to improvise. We learned to be quite resourceful.

Our farmstead was a sandy one. Tools left in the open were soon buried when the wind blew, making their retrieval all the more difficult. But by the time I was five or six, Dad relied on me to keep track of them, and one of my jobs was to pick up after him as he worked. "Go get that wrench," or "Find the hammer," were familiar orders.

He preferred to wait until the beginning of the next season to prepare the big machinery, rather than "put it to bed" correctly at the end of the last one. Consequently, our equipment always needed last-minute repairs.

When I was older, I made sure at the end of the season that at least the plow lathes were greased, so they wouldn't rust. Eventually, I took over the shop and organized it.

Our company shop today reflects that education. The tools are color-coded so, after use, they can be put back in their own designated spot. "A place for everything and everything in its place" is always a good practice: you don't waste time retrieving things.

When it was rainy and we couldn't get into the fields, Dad would do repair work in the shop. I loved those days working with him. He taught me how to saw wood and how to fit it and how to shingle buildings. We even put up an entire building ourselves.

I didn't have much choice; we all helped. When electricity finally came to our area in 1944 or '45, I helped string the wire for it on our farm. Once we had electricity, we could have a pressure pump, which brought up water from the well, so we didn't have to rely on a windmill.

We dug a well house and put in the pump. Then we had to lay a pipe from the well to the house. And when we put in a kerosene water heater, we laid pipe for it, too.

I learned a lot about planning and systems by helping on projects like that. We did most things ourselves, only occasionally hiring experts when we couldn't justify the expense of special tools or when we didn't have the knowledge to do the job right.

Plan Your Work; Work Your Plan

Two machinists who worked side by side in my shop had opposite approaches to any task they undertook. One would start making parts immediately, thinking it out as he went along. He would have completed a large part of his project before the other guy even picked up a piece of metal to be machined; at first glance, he seemed to be the faster worker.

The second machinist sat for a long time, thinking through how he was going to do the project. He assembled all the tools and raw materials he was going to need. When he finally started on the physical job, he went about it smoothly and purposefully, with better quality and less wear on the tooling and machinery. He seemed to have anticipated potential problems and considered options that might make the job easier.

You're probably ahead of me by now: Yes, he consistently finished first. It's a classic tortoise-and-hare story, I suppose, but my point is, because the second machinist took the time to think through the project, he needed less time in which to complete it. Indeed, in many cases, the planning is the hard part.

Unfortunately, in the impatience to get started on a job or to look or feel as if you're accomplishing something, planning is often overlooked. Many workers, to my frustration, tend to open the paint can and dip their brush, only to find out the surface to be painted needs to be prepared.

Gather Information

The result of planning should be a critical path to your goal, so that you eliminate all extraneous elements. The goal might be as simple as catching a plane flight.

Years ago, I was traveling home from Alaska by air. I had packed in my carry-on bag a can of bear-repellent pepper spray I'd been carrying in the wilderness, unaware the spray wasn't allowed in the plane cabin. Of course, the security guard at the checkpoint found it, and I was removed from the check-through line. Bear-repellent pepper spray was a new product at the time, and the security people hadn't seen it before. I spent the next hour or so explaining to several guards why I had it, because they considered it a weapon.

By chance, I'd arrived extra early at the airport, so I didn't miss my plane. But had I stopped for coffee and a magazine, had I ambled through the terminal, I probably would have. My critical path was a beeline to the security gate, before I did anything else. The experience taught me to focus on my goal and to get on the other side of critical elements – in this case, security check-through – before doing anything unrelated.

But before you can apply a critical path, you first have to gather information about your project, especially if it's a complicated one. What do you want to do? What do you have to learn to be able to manage the outcome? Try to think of all the variables. Then assign them to one of two groups: internal procurement and external procurement. Assess your resources for taking care of the internal issues.

Then gather information about the external ones. You may have to go to several sources for the external information and the external activities, and you have to consider that added complexity in the planning phase.

You may be able to start the project without all the information, but gathering the rest of it becomes one of the requisite steps to completion.

Once you've answered those questions from your preliminary research, try to define clearly each role, including yours, in the project. Consider how long completion will take, how much money it will take, and whether you can plan it out reasonably on a calendar and achieve it.

After you've established the workloads and looked at the complexity of the project, consider whether the project is worth all the effort. Do you really want to put your time and money into it? If you do, what is the likelihood of success?

As you study your project, remember, too, to place it in the context of the bigger picture. For example, if you're building a house, you'd better find out whether the supply of roofing materials is adequate for the local housing industry or whether a shortage is in the offing. You might have to change the timing or the sequence of supply orders. If you don't order the roofing materials further in advance, maybe even ahead of the concrete block for the footing, you may sit there waiting, until snow falls and you can't finish the job until next spring.

The topic of critical path planning and management is too big to cover here in detail. In fact, whole books are devoted to it and, of course, you can find information about it on the Internet.

Bottlenecks

Consider a shapely wine bottle. Its narrow neck restricts the flow of the wine as you pour, enabling you to manage the allocation of your precious resource. In production, bottlenecks are not beneficial features, because they restrict the flow of work and interfere with productivity. As a result, they delay the completion of projects and reduce your profit.

Trying to figure where bottlenecks are likely to occur on a project is an important part of planning. The ongoing effort to reduce their effect as you discover them is part of managing.

Let's say you're going to build a machine, and, at a crucial point in the process, you need to have an electronic device installed on it. The installation requires the services of a person with a specialized talent, and nothing else can proceed until that person completes the installation. You have a potential bottleneck. What do you do?

I try to reduce the downtime of waiting for that expert to do his job. I go to the shop and ask how many days it's going to be before the crew needs the electronics person. "Three weeks," they might say. With that information, I start a countdown, and I check with the electronics person about his schedule. Is he going to be on vacation that week?

This is where many people make a big mistake: They know about the timeframe, but they don't keep in touch with the vendor. What happens to the profit margin when they have to pay workers for a week of waiting while that expert is on a fishing trip?

As the countdown continues, I keep everyone informed: "It's two weeks and a day. How are things going?" I make reports to people: "We're on line." It gets down to the scheduled hour, and the electronics person arrives on time with his tools, his parts, his supplies. He has arranged time for the project, and there are no surprises for anyone. We've reduced downtime to a minimum.

It's so simple, yet managers get blindsided by the unexpected, because they don't communicate their needs ahead of time and because they don't keep in touch with others about the production process. Let people know what you know. Sharing information on every project is part of managing bottlenecks and, consequently, increasing productivity.

Prevention

Businesses fail when they are overwhelmed by the problems of yesterday or today. They also can fail because they don't anticipate tomorrow's problems. Good managers are always pondering the question: "What will I do if X happens?" Armed with scenarios, they then can look at ways to prevent a problem, to cope with inevitability, or to create new opportunity.

A certain amount of negative thinking is good. I call it looking on the dark side. If you consider awful possibilities, you can institute measures preventing their occurrence. I have spent hours thinking of all the things that could happen to my business, and I continue to do so. As a result, I have plans for all kinds of disasters, financial and otherwise.

As the steward of the business, as the provider of livelihoods for your employees, you owe it to your workers to keep their welfare in mind as you devise your strategies. Any disaster that affects you affects your employees as well. Of course, they will worry about whether their jobs are at stake.

Before you decide anything, you want to know your options and how they will affect you and your company. Use your consultants. Have your accountant research the tax consequences. Consult with attorneys who specialize in the issues you are considering: lawsuits, pension issues, divorce.

Remember that ounce of prevention and put agreements in place that specify who will do what concerning the company's assets, should a traumatic event occur. It is far easier to negotiate a reasonable solution when all parties involved, spouse and partners, for example, are on speaking terms.

Considering what could happen and then planning for its possibility means it won't run you down like a train coming from the "other" direction. For years, while continuing to hope for the best, I have been planning for the worst. At the same time, hashing out "what-if" scenarios has helped us move successfully into new markets and new products and is one of the reasons we have grown.

Smoke Trails

I was flying on a commercial airliner home to Omaha, Nebraska, and we were over cloud cover as far as I could see. But I knew we were near St. Joseph, Missouri, and I could tell where Omaha was, because I could see the smoke from all the power plants along the Missouri River, rising above the cloud layer. I could pinpoint our location because I knew where those power plants were.

Keep Looking for Clues

It's the same with business. Before you set a goal, you first have to know where you are. So a manager looks for the smoke trails, the clues. What is my market and how is it changing? How good is the national economy?

How's the sales staff doing? What information are they bringing back? What's my production staff doing? What are their capabilities? Are my workers better or worse than they were a year ago? How much can I expect from them?

Administratively, are we counting our bucks correctly? Is the inventory correct? Does the building need painting? Does the roof leak?

Our business history provides us with patterns of process, more smoke trails. If I'm selling so many pounds of 2 x 2 x 1/4-inch 304 stainless-steel angle iron, and I'm starting to order it once every two weeks, I should lay in a bigger inventory of it, so I don't have to order as frequently and so I don't miss sales by running out of stock. On the other hand, it's good to know whether the 4,000 pounds we sold all went to one order. When we restock, we keep in mind that such a sale likely was a one-time event.

Probably the most important concern is the big picture: the history of what you have been able to get out of the marketplace when your industry was at the same level of health as it is now and the national economy was at the same level of health as it is now.

You have to ascertain how much of the market you have, how much your competitors have, where you should be in relation to them, and how hard it is going to be to grow your share of the market. All this is part of the ongoing research that helps you set realistic business goals.

Strategic Planning

I find it helpful to think of life, as well as projects, in terms of time lines. Plotting where you want to be at certain points in life, whether in your personal life or in the life of your company, provides a great overview for making plans. Granted, you might change your ideas – in fact, you probably will – but you at least will have a basis for developing a strategy to accomplish your goals.

The process of making plans that take your business into the future encompasses many elements. Some of them will be similar to those of other companies. Others will be unique to your particular circumstances. We can't cover all of them here, but we can discuss some general areas that are important to consider.

One of them is risk. If your company is in a high-liability industry, can you change direction or move into other ventures to reduce or offset that liability? Likewise, before you expand your business or change direction, look at your potential exposure to liability in the new venture. If risk will increase, can you sufficiently offset it with profit?

Another area is cost. Looking at your book of business and ranking the products and services it encompasses by levels of expense will give you a good idea of where expansion might be most profitable. The part of your business with a history of the greatest costs may not be the segment to grow, unless you can get a premium on the products or services in it.

In the same vein, can you reasonably project the assets you will need? Do you have the employees for what you want to do, or can you get them?

Think about restrictions on your situation. There might be zoning laws that determine how you can or can't expand. There might be other regulations, tax issues, the size of your lot, neighbors who would object – create your own list of limitations. (Call in the consultants.)

Timing is an important consideration. We were a little company with just 25 employees when I bought a huge and expensive machine for our shop. The economy was in a slump, and the big manufacturers weren't spending money. That's the only reason the vendor talked to me.

But because a lot of my strategic planning concerns increasing our capability, I already had gathered the data with which to make my case. I proved we were a successful company and a customer worthy of being taken seriously.

Timing also determined our recent venture into a new market. I tracked the steel-fabricating companies in the red-meat processing industry for several years before we entered it. I knew it would fit my inventory, my skills, and my familiarity with food processing.

But I waited, because those steel-fab companies were beating each other up so badly that pricing was awful. With low margins because of the intense competition, the companies always seemed to be using the next job to cover the costs of the last one. So they were always one job behind on profitability.

I knew that system was going to catch up with them. When we saw them going down for the final count, we hired the best people we could get in the industry and started accessing it. It's now a growing part of our business.

Make the Most of Setbacks

The difficulties and challenges – even the pleasures – of life can distract you if you don't have purposes toward which to direct your effort and attention. Setting goals, even though they might be short term or temporary, gives you a heading, so you don't wander aimlessly from issue to issue or become hindered by setbacks.

I once had a long-term illness that put my career on hold. But because I already had a goal, I could spend my time productively. Even as sick as I was, I used my recovery to study. Once I was able to return to work, I hit the ground running, because I had acquired the knowledge I needed.

A recession is another setback. But you don't have to just wait it out if you have a goal. You can use the slowdown to do important things you can't afford to do any other time. During one recession, we did a lot of building maintenance and employee training. And we tried jobs we otherwise wouldn't have tried because they were more difficult or more labor-intensive or more time-consuming or required higher technical skills.

Once we even learned about manufacturing egg-processing equipment. A worker could spend all day on a project that accounted for a pound or less of material, so I wasn't risking a lot in materials, and I had excess labor available. But because of our research and experimentation during that recession, I decided I didn't want to build egg-processing equipment. I found it far too labor-intensive to be profitable for us, even in good economic times.

Your Continuing Education

The one with the answers is the one with the power. So, to stay on top of things, managers must always be learning. They get information from all kinds of sources, especially the employees, and they study continually. Knowing more increases your influence not only with your employees but also with your customers. When I have succeeded, it's because I have had the information.

For example, a manufacturer had been buying expanded metal from other suppliers and having problems trying to manufacture a product from it. (Expanded metal is a sheet of flat metal that has been slit all over and stretched apart to form a pattern of diamond-shaped openings. It's used for many applications, including metal picnic tables, partitions, and safety barriers.) If the metal didn't break in the fabrication process, it broke when the end user tried to put the finished product into action.

The manufacturer came to me seeking help. He had a backlog of orders, because he was having so much trouble in the fabrication process. I was able to help him because, as part of my constant research of businesses I might want to be in, I had learned about how expanded metal is made, and I knew things even other metal distributors didn't know.

"You can't order for the cheapest price; you have to order with specifications," I told him. "You have to request that the expanded metal be manufactured with the grain of the sheet metal as it comes off the rolling mill, and you have to request that it be made out of a softer steel, so it isn't brittle."

Problem solved, customer gained, because I knew about expanded metal and because I took the trouble to learn about this manufacturer's particular fabrication process and what he needed to do it right.

Study Time

Think of time as a pie. We slice our time pie into many different activities, allotting so much time for the necessities, as well as the niceties, of our life. There's personal time – sleeping, eating, grooming, and the like. There's family time, social time, chores, recreation, career.

The wise person allots a slice of time for study and for developing talents. Whether through a formal continuing-education program or a self-designed process, setting aside time for enhancing our abilities and for accumulating what writer George Will calls "intellectual capital" helps us prepare for opportunities that broaden our lives and our outlook.

In fact, it broadens the scope of opportunities that come to us. In many ways, we create our own futures, because what we do in the years ahead and how successfully we do it will be influenced greatly by the talents and the intellectual capital we have acquired along the way.

Between the ages of 25 and 50, I spent probably 15 hours a week studying. I took materials to study home from the office. I took classes, attended seminars, and read books and magazines. All that time and money were well spent. But to study effectively, you have to know what to study. Talking to others who understand your industry can help you figure out what you need to learn.

Some questions to consider are:

What do I need to know to be better at what I do?

How can I be more effective?

Would understanding other processes in my industry help me manage my workers more effectively?

Magazines are a great source of current information. While I was developing my career, I read up to 40 magazines a month. For instance, doing research into the hot-dip galvanizing process prompted me to buy my company in the first place.

While I was studying that topic, I discovered that the U.S. Department of Agriculture was going to try harder to get people in the food industry to use stainless steel rather than hot-dipped galvanized materials. I learned that metalworking in stainless steel was going to grow because of new laws.

That bit of study led me to take a path different from the one I had anticipated, which was to start a galvanizing operation.

When I bought the company, I studied such topics as accounting, how to do reports, and what kind of format would make information about the company easier for me to understand. I studied machinery and systems that would enhance our capability. I researched markets in which we could work.

By corresponding with authors whose articles I read, I learned more. I have even hired people about whom I read to do seminars for our staff.

As you gain knowledge about a subject, you also gain credibility in the eyes of those who have information you seek. That credibility gives you access to more information.

For example, when I was researching the prospect of buying a boat, I studied boats for a long time. And when I met the owner of a boat that interested me, I was able to talk in terms of his Seaton-designed boat. I understood who the designer was. I knew some things about his style, what his background was, the fact that he really wasn't a marine engineer, but more of a real designer.

The owner was willing to show me through his own boat and to spend time with me. He even talked to me about the problems he'd had working with this particular designer.

A complete stranger invited me aboard and talked to me because I had enough knowledge of his subject. Had I simply been able to compliment him on his pretty blue boat, we likely never would have struck up an acquaintance. My learning curve would have been too steep to interest him.

Research Fundamentals

Research requires, above all, patience. You have to build a good foundation for the knowledge you're seeking. When I look into a project, say, building a machine, there are things I want to know before I start asking questions of the experts.

Until I know enough to make sense of what I'm told, the only question I ask of an authority is: Where do I go to get information? I don't ask questions about specifics until I myself know more.

I use that strategy for several reasons. One, knowing the background helps you ask the necessary questions in an intelligent pattern and make sense of the answers you get.

Two, knowing the background helps you retain knowledge better by providing a context for the information you gather.

Three, knowing the background improves your credibility with the experts, who can tell you've taken the trouble to do your homework in preparation for your interview with them.

Four, knowing the background dictates that you deserve to have the information, that you're serious.

And by the way, people also will be much more interested in talking with you if they see they, too, might have something to gain from you – a potential sale, perhaps, or a consulting contract.

So I start with history. In a new industry, generally, there is a "father" of that industry. Who is that person? Who are the main players? I want to know not about just one person who was in the business, but about four or five people. Are any of them still involved in the industry or the project? Why did they take the approach they took?

For example, did need play a part? Many a machine-shop tool was made by a manufacturer who developed it because the company needed that kind of tool to do a job. Necessity is the mother of invention, after all.

How is the industry, the project, the machine evolving? What is its probable future? Many manufacturing companies have been spun off by people who bought the rights to produce machines.

The next most important thing you can learn after history is the jargon of the industry. Only after you become conversant should you start talking to people in that field.

I studied metal-cutting lasers for a long time, starting with the inventor, because I thought they might be useful in my company. I eventually concluded that the laser was too costly for the benefit it provided and that other processes better satisfied our needs.

I studied lasers more than 15 years ago, but every so often, I send some of my people into the marketplace to see if some of the weaknesses of laser technology have been corrected, so that incorporating the laser into our business might yet be possible.

Decisions

Many people respond to problems with what seem to be gut reactions. When you ask them how they made their decision, they can't tell you. They don't have a rationale or a philosophy on which to base their decisions. They don't have a process by which to make decisions. And they don't know – and haven't considered – how a decision will affect other aspects of their lives. If it turns out badly, they attribute it to bad luck.

The Decision-Making List

Structure can help you make decisions. Don't just think about your concerns; write them down, so you can see them and put them in a logical sequence. This written list will prompt questions you should consider before making a decision. For example, you might be concerned with how your decision will affect your vendors, customers, employees, and community.

Each of those four concerns might branch off into other lists of criteria, such as the effects of your decision in the short term, the intermediate term, and the long term. Some decisions are good for now, but they are lousy for the intermediate future and devastating for the long term. That doesn't mean you shouldn't make the decision; but at least you are aware that, at some point, you will have to reverse it.

Then you will need to create another list for the reversibility of the decision and the consequences of reversing it.

As you get answers to your questions, check off each item. You'll gain confidence in the correctness of your decision, because you will have thought out the ramifications of your choices, rather than mentally just flipped a coin.

Not Quick Decisions But Timely Ones

Don't make a decision until you have to. I don't mean you should delay a decision until a crisis occurs; but many times, events change or facts come to your attention that would render a decision, made earlier, inappropriate. Wait until you have to decide, so you have allowed as much time as possible for the unfolding of circumstances and the gathering of information.

Similarly, before you react to a problem, especially with the "outside world," call together a team of advisers to discuss it. That may be your management team, consultants, or perhaps trusted employees or a friend or two, depending upon the situation. Put more than just your brain to work on a solution. The perspective, the logic, the options others suggest can help you craft the most appropriate action to take.

You might learn new details about the situation, altering your initial interpretation. Above all, don't react in an emotional state, when your thinking is clouded.

Timely or not, don't base a decision on chitchat. Here's the distressing scenario: You are thinking about carrying a new product line, or even going into business, and so, you ask acquaintances and business associates, "If I stock this product (or start this company), would you buy from me?"

You hear, "Yeah, sure, that's a great idea." Based on all the positive responses, you invest a considerable amount in new inventory or a new business, only to find, on your first sales calls, that your friends aren't interested: "Well, I don't really need anything, but if I did, I'd buy from you." Or, "Well, gee, we already have a good, steady supplier, and I can't just dump our usual vendor for no reason."

They're sorry; you're sorrier. It happens. Base your decisions on real market research and serious criteria.

The Difficulties of Decision Making

As a manager, continually being on the hot seat gets to you after a while, even though you enjoy running things. Taking the blame for decisions people don't like or facing the disappointment of people whose requests you refuse puts heavy pressure on a person concerned about what others think and feel.

At the same time, decisions made without criteria against which to measure them might appear arbitrary or personal.

My solution is a simple one: I turn to my consultants – my accountants and my attorneys. They help me develop policies that guide my decision making. By saying, for example, "Our attorney says our policy should be...," I indicate that my answer is based on an authority whose opinion should be respected, and I demonstrate that my reply is objective, fair, consistent, and responsible.

Chapter 5
Efficiency

I *was in 4-H. The county fair was coming up in about a month, and my dad was hounding me to get my calf, my 4-H project, trained to halter-lead. The judges look at how well you manage the animal – or whether, instead, the animal manages you.*

I weighed probably 60 or 70 pounds. The last thing I wanted to do was have a tug of war with a 400-pound calf that had been running wild in the pasture most of the summer. I hated the thought of such an encounter: pulling on the calf's halter, trying to get the animal to come along, pulling, pulling, while the calf, oblivious to my commands, alternately stood rooted as a redwood, then plunged into me, stepping on my foot or knocking me down.

Trying to negotiate with a big animal is a humbling, frustrating experience. The animal wins – unless you come up with more brute force.

So I sat down and pondered how to train this calf without going through all the aggravation I'd endured in previous

*years. Time was short, and I was looking for the most effi-
cient way to get the job done.*

*I decided my solution might lie in our Allis-Chalmers
WD45 tractor, which had a hand clutch. If you hook a belt
or a rope on the clutch, you can put the tractor into gear and
control it while standing on the ground. Pull the rope, which
pulls the hand clutch, and the tractor goes forward.*

*So one day, when Dad was off on an errand, I went to the
pasture and cornered my calf. I put a halter on him, tied him
to the back of the Allis-Chalmers, and rigged the clutch with a
rope. Then I jingled the choke chain under his halter. Of
course, that meant nothing to him; he just stood there. I popped
the clutch on the tractor. The tractor started up, the calf
didn't, and the next thing we both knew, he was on his knees.*

*We repeated that set of steps a few times. I'd jingle the
chain and pop the clutch. The tractor would jerk, the rope
would snap taut. And the calf, standing one moment, would
be on his knees the next, dragging behind the tractor.*

*Then, after two or three sessions, the calf made the con-
nection between the sound of the jingle and the pull on the
halter. At last, when I'd jingle the chain and pop the clutch,
which tugged the rope, the calf would start walking. It did-
n't relate the brute force that overwhelmed it to the tractor;
it related the brute force to me. And what ordinarily would
take a month of training sessions was accomplished in but a
few hours.*

Laziness as a Virtue

I'm lazy. I'll do almost anything to avoid monotonous or repetitive
tasks, like training a calf. And if I can't avoid them altogether, I'll look
for ways to do them more easily and more quickly – more efficiently –
than the usual way. Efficiency made bearable a tedious chore like
training an obstinate calf.

In business, as on the farm, it also makes for greater productivity and, therefore, a better bottom line. My "laziness" has made me a better manager. As I develop procedures to enhance our efficiency, I delegate them to somebody else and go on creating solutions to other dilemmas.

Tweak Toward Excellence

Webster's New World Dictionary defines efficiency as "the ratio of effective work to the energy expended in producing it." The quest for efficiency is one of a manager's primary jobs. You have to look at every aspect of your operation and ask the question: How can we make this more efficient? Honing your operation toward the best ratio of efficiency is a priority.

Consider Frank and Lillian Gilbreth, a married team of efficiency experts, who are considered pioneers in industrial-time-and-motion study. Their family life is the subject of the best-selling *Cheaper by the Dozen*, written by two of their 12 children, Frank, Jr., and Ernestine Gilbreth Carey.

As a bricklayer's young helper, just out of high school, Gilbreth, much to the consternation of his foreman, took it upon himself to improve the process of laying bricks. He designed a scaffold that made him the fastest bricklayer.

The foreman duplicated his design for all the other bricklayers and suggested that he submit it to the Mechanics Institute, which awarded it a prize. When others adopted the same methodology, everyone, including the customer, benefited because bricklaying costs dropped.

Gilbreth went on to become a foreman, then a superintendent, then an independent contractor, building bridges and canals, factories and industrial towns. As he continued his quest for efficiency, he was often recruited to refine processes in the factories he helped build. By the time he was 27, he had offices in New York, Boston, and London.

I appreciate his obsession with efficiency. He even reduced the way he handled a bar of soap to a minimum number of moves so he could streamline his bathing. I draw the line short of that, but I do continue to look for ways in which we can enhance the efficiency of our operation. Here are some of the things I've learned.

Time and Money Best Spent

One big way to improve your operation, as Gilbreth did, is by looking at your largest expense and putting your first and best efforts toward making it as efficient and effective as possible.

At our company, it was production, so in earlier years, as manager of only a few employees, I attended to my production staff first. When they were at work, I thought production; everything else was subordinate to that concern. I was constantly in and out of the production room, making sure my workers were making the goods and adding value to the raw materials on a consistent basis, making the most of their time.

Meanwhile, I looked for ways to enhance their production with better machinery and improved procedures.

Focusing on the biggest expense is an example of industrial triage. This ingenious concept arose from the bloody battlefields of the Hundred Years' War (1337-1453), when French physicians realized that indiscriminately trying to treat all the injured, regardless of the seriousness of their injuries, cost the lives of many soldiers who would have survived had they been treated sooner.

Out of this crisis came a process of setting medical priorities: triage. Patients were sorted according to whether they would survive with or without treatment. Those who would survive only with intervention were treated first. Those who were going to survive, even without intervention, were put on the waiting list. Those who were going to die, no matter what the intervention, were simply made comfortable.

Transferring that dilemma to a business, the question becomes: What is the most pressing concern, the one on which a manager should concentrate time and money? Don't waste energy on problems that solve themselves. Don't waste energy on projects that will fail anyway. Indeed, perhaps the biggest challenge a manager faces is to determine what will live and what will die, with and without intervention.

Obviously, this is about setting priorities. What most needs attention? What can be delegated? What can be put off until later? What can be ignored altogether? Most managers tend to focus on urgent rather than vital concerns. Let Mr. Hobbs explain.

Charles R. Hobbs, in an excellent series called *Your Time and Your Life,* unfortunately out of print, used a simple matrix to explain our choices. He suggested that events, situations, and goals in our lives be divided into four categories:

- Vital and urgent, such as responding to an emergency call from home;
- Not vital but urgent, such as answering an insistently ringing telephone;
- Vital but not urgent, such as planning a business expansion;
- Not vital and not urgent, such as cleaning out the supply room.

That which is vital has a high payoff, says Mr. Hobbs, and it is to vital issues and projects we should devote our attention; instead, he points out, it is urgency that more often spurs us to action.

The "ideal" category is "vital but not urgent," what produces success and gives us satisfaction. In setting priorities, keeping the long view in mind will help us shift into that ideal arena, and careful planning will help us do what we need to do toward our priorities in time to avoid the stomach-churning sense of urgency.

Roger Merrill, in his book *Connections,* looks from another perspective at how we should allocate our resources. He suggests we fail at being effective and efficient by not distinguishing between those things that concern us, world hunger, perhaps, and those on which we can have a real and direct effect, such as supporting a local homeless shelter.

Two concentric circles illustrate his point. One, the circle of concern, encompasses all the things on our mind and needing attention — by someone. Inside the circle of concern is a much smaller circle of influence, which comprises only issues for which we actually can make a difference.

Everyone's circle of influence is different, depending upon interests, aptitudes, abilities, and resources. Successful people pick carefully what they're going to do, focusing their efforts where they think they have the greatest chance of success: within their circle of influence.

Thrashing about in a circle of concern, where issues are beyond our control, dilutes our effort and wastes our resources. The result of all our work is disproportionately small. In contrast, we can accomplish much more if we focus on issues within our circle of influence. There, where our capability lies, we get the most for our efforts; we do the most good.

Focus

Focus on what you do best. You should be continually grooming and building on your core of abilities. Rather than try to develop something extraneous to your innate abilities, zero in on your talents and develop them.

My core was business understanding and development, how to supervise people, and other associated topics. I kept working on that core. I didn't go off and take a course in geology, or something like that, although in many cases I was tempted.

Delegate! Delegate! Delegate!

I once met an old couple who had been married 60 years. I asked the husband, "How have you succeeded in your marriage?" He replied, "I let her take care of all the little problems. I take care of the big problems – and I try to make all the big problems little problems."

Help Others Succeed

Successful people learn to delegate so, on the way to their goals, they can move on to other tasks. They can take on more because they enlist others in their efforts. Employees to whom tasks are delegated become more valuable and fulfilled as they learn to do more things. Consequently, they too succeed.

Delegating isn't easy for everybody. In fact, some independent types simply cannot delegate. But most of us can learn how to do it or do it better, and the more you delegate, the easier it becomes.

Some people don't delegate because they can do the job in less time than explaining it to someone else would take. But that's a false economy. A time will come when sequencing all the tasks will overload those nondelegators. Then they will have to delegate and take the time, at that inconvenient point, to explain how to do those tasks. Delegating should be a strategy, not a necessity.

Delegate when you don't have to do it, when you aren't pinched for time and have the leisure to teach someone how to do the task. Then, the next time you're busy and have to have that job done, you can delegate.

How to Delegate

First, look for tasks easy to delegate. In fact, I look at most jobs I'm doing as candidates for delegating and, in doing so, I look for restrictions that might preclude delegating.

For example, some issues such as payroll are confidential; they should be handled only by someone absolutely discreet and trustworthy. In other cases, a project might have too many options to be a good candidate for delegating. Look for tasks that have patterns of procedure easily replicated and monitored.

Failure of a delegated project will make you reluctant to delegate again, so before giving someone a project, understand all the steps it includes. Before I assign a task, I do it myself and work out all the bugs. Then I show the person who's going to do the job how I did it and what the result should be. That person might find another way to do the task, but he knows how I did it and what I expect as a product. Interim steps and products become checkpoints for progress.

If somebody else in your organization is better at a task, admit it and delegate the task to that person. Being willing to admit other people can do some things better than you can is not only an exercise in humility but also a big step toward efficiency. For a simple instance, I don't type letters, even with computer assistance; other people are more competent at that task than I.

If I'm busy doing things other than what I'm good at, which is planning, then the whole group is affected. In fact, I'm doubly inefficient. First, I'm less effective at the task itself; second, I'm not attending to the work I do best to improve the company and enhance our future.

Stay focused on the most important things you can do to make other people's work move forward, to move a project forward, to move the company forward.

Put It on Paper

I often delegate in writing, or I might copy a memo and circle topics of concern I want a person to attend, perhaps numbering them in the order of their importance to me. Especially, I don't delegate a complicated project without writing down an explanation. I keep a written copy of my request, as both a placeholder for me to be sure the work gets done and a reminder to the other person that I will check on his progress.

I think of the process as taking a number in line. If I put my request in writing, I probably will get my project finished sooner than will somebody else who makes only an oral request. Without a tangible reminder, the person who is to do the project is more likely to forget.

All day long we get distracted by demands for our attention: a ringing telephone, lunch break, reports, meetings. But if you've provided a note, then when the person returns to his work after the distracting phone call, there's your written reminder. A written reminder also makes a statement: the issue is important. Many times, watching people direct others orally, I've seen the message shrugged off as inconsequential.

Delegating to Other Businesses

Now, let's consider delegating at the corporate level. An efficient organization is always looking to see if it can accomplish its tasks externally more cheaply than doing the work in-house. Just because your company can do something doesn't mean your company should do it.

Another company may have the equipment, the trained personnel, or the expertise to do it better than your company can. Scrutinize your production for what you could job out.

Look, too, at what your vendors could provide you. Could you "delegate" part of the project to them? Often, buying a value-added component from your vendor would cost you less in the long run than your adding that value. A vendor who really wants to make the sale will try to accommodate you.

As an example, let's say one of my customers requires a big electric motor in a food-production system we're building for him, and he wants a special finish on the motor for critical equipment wash-downs.

I can purchase the motor from one of my vendors, but it has to be painted.

We aren't set up to do that special finish, so painting it ourselves would be more expensive and time-consuming. I ask my vendor if he will do it or will contract it out before delivery from a qualified vendor. He should be willing to paint the motor – add the value our customer wants-as part of his service, to help make the sale to us.

In this case, using a more complete product, even if it costs more, is more cost-effective in the long run than starting with raw goods. We gain time. We gain quality. We gain production on other projects. We can delay paying for that item because we own it for a shorter time before we sell it to our customer.

Asking what your vendor might be able to do for you should be part of the ongoing negotiation process. If you lack enough shelf space, can your vendor hold a product for you until you want it? Can he deliver it when you want it? Can he package it in a special way for you? Will he give you a warranty? If you, as a customer, don't ask for what you really want, you may not get all the value to which you are entitled.

Chain Stitching Procedures and Options

One can evaluate a manufacturing project by asking two questions: Which components, such as steps or materials, are unique? Which components are similar to each other or to components in other projects? Components that are different indicate points at which someone will have to make choices requiring comparison and evaluation, in other words, thought. In building custom-designed machinery, the design process requires a lot of imagination and thought, and aspects of the construction process require such input as well.

Components that are the same every time fall into the category of procedurality. The very nature of a procedure indicates its similarities to previous experiences. Fewer variables and more consistency make for a more predictable outcome. We can repeat experiences. Building custom-designed machines requires such common procedures as shearing and welding, for example.

I create a pie diagram for every project, to indicate which operations are unique and which are similar to each other or, perhaps, to operations we've done on other projects. Then I can communicate better with the people who are going to build the machine: "OK, Leroy, it's like the chicken cooker we built five years ago. Remember how you attached the auger?"

Grouping Like Tasks

Some people seem to work on a basis of happenstance, rather like a bee zigzagging from flower to flower. But if you group similar procedures, such as making all your phone calls at one time, you set up for them only once. You have all the phone numbers at hand, all the return messages in a pile, and all your concentration on the task. That's a simple example. Let's take a bigger one, a building project.

The construction budget for our new 60,000-square-foot building fell short of completing the entire plant. Rather than simply build the size we could afford to finish, then add on later, we completed the external parts of the whole building – the footings, the walls, and the roof, leaving the end of the building unfinished inside. We didn't need electricity or plumbing at that end; we didn't even need a floor.

Just setting up to break ground and build takes major planning – and, therefore, money – whether the project is a new building or an addition. We avoided duplicate start-up costs by grouping work, that is, completing perimeter walls for both the space needed immediately and the additional square footage wanted later.

By eliminating the secondary construction project, we saved at least $100,000 in duplicate start-up charges that would have been incurred by doing two separate projects.

Surprises Are for Birthdays

One of the biggest issues in business is avoiding unpleasant surprises. Control as many variables as you can discover; account for everything you can. Granted, you can't know all the details, but you can develop some control over your circumstances. Why be caught off guard unnecessarily?

That's one reason why procedures and systems are so valuable: They provide predictability and consistency. Measurements are built in; standards are upheld. You know what the results are supposed to be. Such systems free you to move on to optional situations that can't be made systematic and to which you, therefore, have to devote more time and energy.

Creating a procedure or a system that can be repeated for commonly done tasks saves thought and effort and eliminates errors and problems. Much of the value of the computer and its software, for example, lies in systematic programs, which do away with many errors caused by the variables of human input.

Look at an example of a simple system applicable in our work setting. Now, some companies don't mind letting a visitor, such as a regular delivery person, wander through their company. But you should look at anyone coming into your plant as an intrusion into your environment, someone who needs to be monitored.

It isn't that they'll steal something, necessarily, although that could happen. It's that you should be concerned about safety and the disruption of activities.

Today, in my company, I don't worry as much about visitors, because we have in place a system to control them. In addition to a receptionist, who screens visitors and controls a locked door to the office area beyond her desk, we have number pads, requiring codes, at entrances to different areas of the plant to restrict access. And a company representative escorts all visitors; no outsider wanders around alone, even in the break room.

We also have laid out our environment so pick ups and deliveries result in contact with as few of our people as possible. A delivery person allowed to walk through the shop is going to disrupt the work of every person with whom he comes into contact, even briefly. Multiply that moment by several times a day, times a week, times a month... well, I think I've made my point.

Procedures accomplish other ends, too. If you do something the same way every time, you don't have to worry as much about whether it was done right. You have greater confidence in the outcome because you've previously done it that way many times. And you gain credibility, because others know your results are consistently good.

In aviation, one way to ensure procedures are followed accurately and completely is to use checklists. Checklists exist for each aspect of a flight, from the preflight inspection to shutting down the engine. One of the most important ones is the prelanding checklist – B/CGUMPSS, for short, an acronym that stands for:

> **B**oost pump on (for fuel),
> **C**arburetor heat on,
> **G**as (making sure the selector is on the fuller tank),
> **U**ndercarriage (lowering the gear!),
> **M**ixture of fuel set,
> **P**ropeller at high RPM,
> **S**eatbelt secure, and
> **S**peed appropriate.

We do a B/CGUMPSS check on downwind, base, and final approach to the runway, to be sure we have followed the prelanding procedure correctly and we avoid a gear-up landing.

The Danger of Rote

Following a repetitive procedure makes the process seemingly automatic. Indeed, assuming everything will be the same and nothing will go wrong makes it difficult to notice the occasional variation in a routine.

Let's go back to our B/CGUMPSS checklist. During flight reviews, a cagey instructor surreptitiously pulls the circuit breaker for the gear, in which case the gear won't go down when you pull the lever. The purpose of this little trick is to see if the pilot actually is thinking about the checklist or is just going through the motions.

If you're nervous or preoccupied, you might follow the checklist, even saying aloud all the items on the list, yet not confirm that the gear went down by checking the green "gear down" light. You may even "see" the "gear down" light when it isn't on, because you expect to.

The danger of a routine is that it becomes rote performance, and if we aren't looking for differences, we may not see them. Following a procedure does save time and concentration, but we still have to attend to it.

So when there is a variation you want your workers to notice, you'd better exaggerate that variation with the equivalent of red flags, flashing lights, and clanging sirens. Tell them ahead of time if possible. Train them to look for differences.

And be aware that "inclusionary" people, who are inclined to accept situations and people rather than to question them, will find it more difficult to see differences than "exclusionary" types, who don't take anything for granted.

The Efficiency of Quality

When we order new machines or supplies, I encourage employees to look at catalogs to see what's new. Just because we've been using a particular kind of thingamajig for years doesn't mean a better one didn't come onto the market last month. Whether it's an improved copy paper that works better with inkjet printers, or simply mechanical pencils that are less annoying because the lead fills automatically rather than having to be inserted by hand – every little thing has a magnifying effect and should be considered from the standpoint of finding the best tool to do the job.

Even the packaging a product comes in affects the quality of our work, because the packaging may determine how the product is stored or dispensed. How well we do our jobs and the quality of the products we manufacture, as well as how efficiently we can make them, depend upon the products and tools we use.

Cost-Benefit Analysis of Improving Efficiency

How do you know whether an upgrade for efficiency is worth its cost? Most technical improvements fall under the category of economic value. We ask whether we are going to get a return on investment. That return on investment generally comes from reducing the time it takes to do a job, as well as from reducing frustration.

For example, if you buy a piece of equipment that saves five hours a week and your time burden is $25 per hour, then you have a $125 weekly payback for buying that equipment. If it costs $1,000, you'll receive your entire payback in eight weeks.

Even if you can't justify a purchase economically, there may be some intrinsic value to consider. The initial outlay for duplicate equipment and materials at each workstation, for example, might be offset by the ease and convenience that result, the savings of time and effort, the elimination of lost tools and frustration.

An upgrade might improve the overall quality of your product. For instance, a new printer for producing an instruction booklet for a piece of equipment you've sold a customer may not print any faster, but the quality of its product may make the booklet easier to read and more professional-looking. That in itself might, in the long run, be an investment in marketing.

You can try to find a bunch of marketing projects to justify the printer, but look at how many things in your daily activities, if improved, reflect a marketing value. You probably can justify taking a little out of your marketing budget to buy this printer.

Upgrading phone systems may be justifiable, on the basis of not only cost savings but also marketing value, because the phone system is the first line of marketing. It's a marketing tool in both the sales and purchasing departments. It's a marketing tool for everyone in the company who uses it. If the phone system irritates the caller because it doesn't work well, it's hurting your business.

Perhaps a new machine can help you improve communications. A new printer with better graphics might eliminate errors between the engineering department and the shop. Even a fax machine that makes clearer copies might smooth the process of ordering materials.

Continually look for ways to improve the processes and the equipment you use. Whereas you previously did a task weekly, you might do it four times a week now. The equipment you could justify for doing the task four times a week might be completely different from the equipment you used for the weekly task. But if it saves you time, it enhances your efficiency, which, in turn, enhances your bottom line.

Shipping and Receiving

Think of your shipping and receiving department as a line of defense for controlling quality. At our company, delivery trucks don't just back up to our dock and dump off the merchandise. Someone attends to them from the moment they arrive, and everything we receive is checked against the manifest and the purchasing slip to make sure what we got is what we agreed to.

We train our people to check things out. We teach them that verifying orders and checking for defective parts are crucial to our success. Our system of verifying orders includes giving our truck drivers cell phones, so they can keep in communication with us. If they have any question, they get right on their own phone and call; they don't have to stand around waiting for permission from a vendor or a customer to use the phone. Better to make a phone call if they suspect there's a problem than to return with the wrong item.

Whether picking up or delivering, we make sure we get the right item, the right quantity, and the right quality. And if there's the slightest damage, we note it immediately on the receiving tickets.

A friend of mine, who was fabricating parts for us, once gave me a great compliment. "Parks," he said, "your truck driver came over nicely dressed. He had a clipboard. He walked in, said he was there to pick up the piece you'd ordered, and asked if it was ready."

My friend continued: "And then he carefully inspected what he was to take back, loaded it, and left. I was impressed with his professionalism."

Then, he said, "Ron, if I'd sent my driver to you, you could have thrown a dead horse in the back of the truck and he'd have brought it back to me."

I was proud of my employee, but he was just doing his job as trained.

The Importance of Estimating

A truck driver in line at a weigh station watched a man in the passenger seat of the truck ahead of him, which was on the scales, crawl out of the cab and inch his way back to the van. Clinging to the side of the rig with one hand, the man furiously beat the wall of the van with his other fist.

The driver of the second truck, succumbing to curiosity, walked up to the first truck and asked the guy what he was doing. "Overweight on canaries," the man replied. "Gotta keep 'em flying."

Obviously, he was trying to skew the weight estimate. Well, it's only a little stretch to the real message here, which is that estimating is an important component of efficiency.

Hauling a Philodopus

Estimating helps you determine, first, whether you should do a project. Suppose someone asked you to haul a "philodopus" to Philadelphia. If you said yes before you knew what a "philodopus" was, you could be in for a great adventure. Is it as big as an elephant or as small as a shrew? Are you going to have to rent a big truck, or can you take it in a Toyota Tercel? Do you have to feed it hundreds of bales of hay or a few pellets of pet food? How far is Philadelphia anyhow?

To plan a project well, cover costs, and make a decent profit, you must be able to visualize the scope of the task you are to perform. You have to know its volume, for one thing, its weight, its costs, its quality, perhaps even its delicacy. If you don't know about those aspects of the project, you can't possibly develop a close estimate, and you quite probably won't make a profit.

Even with a project similar to one you've already done, consider the elements that are different. A project differing only slightly in finished size or weight from an earlier project might require hugely different methods of handling during processing because of that small variation. Inches and ounces do matter.

Estimating helps you set parameters for a project, so you can build in a contingency safety margin of more cash, more people, or outsourcing possibilities. Estimating also helps you set benchmarks, so you can keep track of where you are in the process.

It's like taking off in an airplane. I project down the runway where my plane should lift off. If it isn't airborne by that point, I pull the throttle and shut down, because something is wrong. If I didn't have that takeoff spot in mind, I could drive the plane right off the end of the runway by being too slow to lift off yet too fast to stop short.

In business, you measure your progress, and even if you don't achieve what you thought you should at a certain point, you can see what you've gained. Then you can determine why you didn't get as far as you thought you would. Do you have enough resources for the project? Were your projections correct? If the estimate was wrong, why was it wrong? What resources are available for going on? Is the project worth continuing?

Unless you keep track of your costs, you can't know any of this. Constantly recording the actual costs of each project will refine your estimates to greater accuracy.

Tell It Like It Really Is

Clear communication is a cornerstone of efficiency. And it's fundamental to safety. If we aren't all speaking the same language and using the same industry jargon in a workplace, we can't possibly get and give appropriate information. How can we do a good job in a Tower of Babel?

Bolts or Cap Screws?

When I took over our company, the shop had no common vernacular. One person's "bolt" was another's "cap screw." Is this a big deal? Well, a bolt is a cap screw with a nut on it. If I order 150 cap screws, I need 150 nuts, but if I ask for 150 3/4-10 hex bolts, the nuts are included. So one of the first things I did as the new owner was to establish a common jargon. We went back to basics, with labels and training, until we had a common language we could use to convey the correct information. In manufacturing, especially, it's important to say what you mean. A bolt is not a cap screw.

First, the Deal Breakers

When I had to find a new insurance company, I let underwriters I was interviewing know up front that our old insurance company had dropped us and why. (We were in an industry for which the insurance company had incurred such high costs that it eliminated businesses in that industry from its customer list.) "Do you have any further interest?" I asked each of them. If they didn't want my business, I didn't want to waste our time answering a detailed list of questions.

Don't wait until the end of the discussion to bring up "surprises," and don't keep people in the dark about deal breakers. If you know of an issue that will come up with a project, warn the other person. For one thing, if you say something, the issue may not become a problem. If you don't, the project could cost more when the issue has to be dealt with unexpectedly.

For another thing, people appreciate being treated honestly and with respect. And they are entitled to decide based on the whole picture, not your edited version of it.

Paperwork

Communicating on paper efficiently also presents its challenges. Never mind that filling out forms is the symbol of bureaucracy at its worst. A form is an excellent means of conveying information, but only if the form itself is in a useable format rather than a haphazard bunch of questions.

For instance, we developed a form for doing estimates that fits our particular quoting process. It expresses clearly the information people who are associated with the project need to do their jobs. Workers can understand the estimate quickly and accurately. They can see the history of the quoting process on a project and what the job will entail. Valuable information isn't overlooked because somebody forgot to ask the question or forgot to write down the answer.

Don't make your people have to conform to the forms. Tweak those paper instruments so logic and sequence, order and rationale are obvious to the reader, so the form serves your purposes, rather than the other way around. Develop a format that gives your people the answers they need to do their jobs for you.

Speaking of interoffice communication, let's hear it again for the computer. It's a great tool for communicating, whether through e-mail for a quick turnaround or through software that enables the transfer, duplication, or manipulation of information.

But transferring paperwork is another matter. A vinyl "sleeve" with a clear cover is great for that process as well as for holding papers on your desk. Vinyl sleeves keep unrelated papers separate, and you can see immediately what's inside without having to open them to look. We use them for short-term transfer and retrieval.

We use labeled manila folders filed alphabetically for longer-term storage and retrieval.

Documenting

Information is one of your most valuable commodities, and documentation, however tedious, is a vital aspect of business. Even seemingly trivial information could help you in negotiations. I learned those lessons well while I was working for the company at which I learned the basics of the steel-fabricating business.

We frequently received railroad shipments of steel, and the bills always seemed to be for more pounds than we'd ordered. I started keeping track of the date we placed each order and the gross weight we ordered, and I began challenging the bills.

Once we could produce evidence of the actual weight we ordered, it was amazing how the weight charged on the bills came closer to the actual weight of the shipments.

Keeping good records helped me convince my banker to reduce my loan interest rate and to extend the terms of my loans. I was able to present data showing my bank's low level of participation in all the loans I successfully had procured from various sources. I also was able to illustrate the low risk my company presented to the bank's loan portfolio.

The way you document directly affects your efficiency. It will determine whether, for example, you can go immediately to the records of a phone conversation you had regarding your insurance policy or whether you will waste precious time scrounging for a scrap of paper you used for taking notes and then threw onto a scrap pile of paper, along with journals, newspapers, reports, and memos.

I have standardized my documentation process after such frustrating experiences and several experiments. I keep a standard-sized notebook by the phone for taking notes as I talk. It has perforated, three-hole, lined 8-1/2-x-11-inch paper. I use the same kind of notebook to document conversations and meetings and to send handwritten memos. No little scratch pads, except, I admit, I've been known to use paper napkins during chats over drinks or dinner.

I put only one discussion topic on a page, leaving enough room to add related information. Another topic, another page. As cheap as paper is, there's no need to squeeze a bunch of unrelated notes onto a single page. How are you going to file that piece of paper so all the information is retrievable? You can't. How much time is it going to take to recopy the notes so you can file them separately? Too much.

Each project gets its own binder, in which I collect memos and notes on everything concerning that project, whether it's a building, a trip, or information regarding my aviation medical certificate. In the front of that binder, I write questions or topics about which I want to know more, and I check them off as I learn what I want to know about them.

The process of accomplishing things is getting all the questions answered.

Saving on Insurance

We've saved thousands of dollars in insurance costs over the years, by researching the criteria insurance companies use to determine premiums and then preparing a report showing how those criteria apply to our business. Here's our story.

I hadn't owned the company long before I got a call one day from our insurance company. They were dropping us, effective immediately, because we were in a category of businesses considered too risky or too costly for them to insure. In fact, they washed their hands of us so thoroughly that they even returned our premium.

They'd given me no warning or waiting period. And I'd given them no trigger event, such as a claim, to justify their abrupt action against me. So I was able to negotiate another 30 days of coverage, to give me time to get a policy from another company.

I set to work, using my file of business cards of insurance representatives who'd stopped by. I found an underwriter willing to work with me, and I asked him: "What have you learned over the years about how insurance companies look at businesses? What do we need to tell these people?" And I created a team to work on the problem.

I realized insurance companies rate a category of businesses based on the worst case in that category. I had to show we weren't a worst-case company.

Yes, we're a manufacturer of food-processing equipment, and that means we make equipment that cuts, grinds, mashes, and can hurt people. But I knew that, of all the equipment we make and all the activities we perform, only a small percentage of our business is at that level of liability, so our premium shouldn't be based on total exposure to extreme liability.

I created a classification system sorting the different kinds of work we did by how much risk was involved, and I rated every job that went through our engineering department by that job's potential liability. Whether it was designed by the customer to be produced by us or whether we designed and built it, whether it was mechanical or hydraulic or electrical, these and several other criteria helped me index the level of our potential liability.

Second, because insurance premiums are charged per $1,000 in sales, I looked at how our sales figures broke out in each class of risk. We shouldn't be charged a high-risk premium for the materials-distribution side of our business.

Third, I created a strong safety program and improved the quality of the workplace as preventive measures.

With the help of our insurance agent, who is a general underwriter, we made a good case and got a policy at a reasonable rate. After we'd been doing this classification system for four or five years, I talked to a representative of a company almost identical to ours and asked him what their rates were. We were doing four times as much business, and they were paying twice as much for insurance.

It took hours to collect that information, and it took hours to develop that report, but the documentation continues to pay off.

On the Phone

Don't waste phone calls. Even if the person you reached can't help you – "Sorry, we don't carry that item" – try to get additional information that makes the call worthwhile: "Can you recommend another distributor?"

When I talk on the telephone, I write down at least the name of the person and the date and time, so I'll have a reference if I have to call back for clarification, such as for an order or an appointment. At the end of the call, I may throw away the paper, if there's no further need for it, but I start with at least this minimal information until I see where the call is going to go. Even the name of a receptionist or a sales clerk might be helpful if you have to backtrack.

A machine distributor taught me about keeping phone notes. He used steno pads, keeping a record of every phone call he made or received. On the front of each pad, he wrote the beginning and ending dates of the time span that was covered. He had stacks of those pads, and he could find in them the notes from conversations he'd had five years earlier.

With everything he needed to know about an order at hand, he'd take the steno pad with him to the shipping and receiving department and arrange for the order. He didn't try to do things from memory. Rarely did he ship anything wrong. He was a great vendor.

Get Organized

A discussion of efficiency wouldn't be complete without talking about staging, queuing, storing, and retrieving. When we looked at the production process in our company with these concepts in mind, we found many ways to improve. We put our manufacturing processes in order, so everything flows "downstream" to shipment of the product. We created decentralized storage areas, so each operations area has its own preprocess stage, queue, and store zones and its own postprocess stage, queue, and store zones.

Generally, if your layout is logical, the "postprocess" zones for one process are the "pre-process" zones for the next.

Using a specially designed forklift that runs on an electronic metal strip, we created a retrieval system to move materials from one area to another. The overall system we developed, called Physically Integrated Manufacturing (PIM), reduced our production costs immensely.

With the increased efficiency, we recovered the upgrading and installation costs of the system in just 30 months. Let me explain the basic components: staging, queuing, and storing.

Staging

Staging refers simply to the flow of work. Let's say we have a project that requires cutting holes out of metal. If we form the metal before we cut the holes, we restrict our options for how we could cut the holes. Proper staging would lead us to set up so we cut the holes, then form the metal. That's putting first things first.

Staging also refers to work stations, where the needed tools and supplies are at hand. Let's take a simple example from home: toasting bread. The toaster is the center of the workstation for that task. It sits on the counter next to the refrigerator, where the butter and jelly are. We keep the bread in the cupboard above the toaster, with some knives and small plates. Everything we need for making toast is within arm's reach.

Likewise, as one simple example in our factory, each workstation has its own color-coded set of tools. Workers don't have to scour the workshop to find a tool somebody else used and didn't return.

Queuing

Queuing, which simply means setting up materials for the next step in the process, happens at two points: immediately before a process and immediately after it. It's easy to overlook queuing as an important part of the workflow, but the way you queue your materials has a direct effect on your efficiency.

Let's say I have in a storage area an inventory of metal sheets, some of which I want to shear up and use in my operation. I retrieve and queue them neatly stacked next to the shear machine. I don't leave them on the forklift or stack them around me on the floor. I have enough room to queue them properly, so moving them into the shear machine takes minimal effort. After I shear them, I have enough space to queue them for the next stage or to store or ship them.

Storing

Storage systems are sinkholes of inefficiency. Lost parts, machinery damaged or broken because it wasn't properly "put to bed," lack of adequate control over inventory, such that duplication, shortages, even theft are chronic issues – poor storage procedures cause all these problems.

Then there is the extra time spent looking for lost items or repairing broken ones. Often, it's the highest-paid person in a shop who tracks down lost parts.

And improperly storing machinery guarantees it will lose value because of damage. What happens to the engine of a lawnmower that sits over the winter with gas in the tank? You might be talking to your friendly lawnmower repairperson the following April.

The time to store something properly is not 10 weeks after you've decided you're not going to use it; the time is immediately.

Consider, too, problems associated with replacing a missing part. Say you need to make 10 little parts and it takes an hour to set up to make those parts. If you lose one of them, setting up to make the single replacement part will take you another hour. Time lost.

Then, the replacement part isn't going to be consistent with the other parts, because every manufacturing lot has the potential to be different. You may have to engineer a slightly different jig for welding on the replacement part.

And, finally, the pairs of parts won't match exactly, so the quality of your product has slipped.

Some Storage Solutions

Having said all that, here are some simple ways to gain control over your storage. First, capitalize on the space you have, both horizontally and vertically. Getting up on a ladder in the factory one day, I really noticed for the first time all the unused space above our heads. We were heating and lighting the whole shop but using only the bottom six feet or so. Today we have vertical shelving units that rise almost to the ceiling throughout the entire factory.

Second, make sure everything is easily retrievable. Don't make it necessary to move one thing to access something else. We ensure accessibility by lining the shelving units along aisles reserved for retrieval. A letter-number system indicating location and shelf height gives every spot in the factory its own address. Upon arrival, all materials are labeled with an address and catalogued in inventory before being sent to their storage spot.

Third, standardize your system both to make retrieval easier and to protect what you are storing. We put our shop inventory and address system on computer. And we installed standard metal shelving throughout the factory.

In the office, we have the usual file cabinets for papers, but we also use my "white-box system" for odd-sized things. Three sizes of white, heavy-duty cardboard boxes accommodate most of what we store. The boxes, the same in length and width but varied in height, stack easily into a common storage system.

We label (in pencil) all the boxes in the same spot on one side and group them by subject. These boxes hold 80 percent of the items I store. I even have a white box for miscellaneous items I simply can't throw away.

Trivial details, you might say, but when you're trying to find something and time is money, such standardization pays off. After all, if you can't retrieve something, it isn't stored; it's lost.

Your Desk as Storage

I try hard to keep my desktop a workplace and not a shelf, but let's face it, at least the perimeter of most desktops, including mine, is a shelf, a place for queuing and staging papers for different processes. One pile is for typing, a second for filing, a third for reviewing.

But for some people, the whole desktop is a storage shelf. Everything goes into one huge pile – or several. Important papers, checks, letters unread and unanswered, all go to Limbo in an undifferentiated pile.

I know someone has a problem when he calls me for information I gave him five days ago because I can retrieve it more easily than he can in his desktop jumble. If information is important enough to keep, it's important enough to store so you can retrieve it.

I'll give you a simple format for making the most of your desk space. Think of your desk as the center of three concentric circles. Keep within arm's reach, circle A, the things you use constantly. In the next larger circle, B, keep those things to which you refer frequently, and in the largest circle, C, store those things to which you only occasionally need access. Consider your desktop, desk drawers, and upper shelves within these circles. You could even apply this concept to the general office.

If you need to call in reinforcements, remember that professional organizers are ready to help. But do it now – the value of their assistance doesn't diminish.

The Fundamental Efficiency

Don't overlook the efficiency of holding on to employees, as well as cross-training them for other jobs in the company. It is expensive – and foolish – to ignore the costs of turnover and retraining.

Every new employee goes through some kind of on-the-job training. It ranges from a simple orientation for a new professional who has been academically trained to a major component of the employee's time at the company, if experience is the more important requirement.

Many employees come to us with perhaps some technical schooling or some experience at another metalworking shop, but for expertise in the kind of custom work that is our specialty, they have to learn a lot on the job with us. We invest considerable time and money in their education, and finding other employees to replace them is difficult and expensive. We want to avoid laying them off, even in bad economic times.

Chapter 6
Creating a Workforce

When I was about eight, Dad hired me out to neighboring ranchers, who harvested prairie hay from their fields to feed their Hereford cattle. In those days, farmers did what was called "exchange work." But the people I worked for never came and worked for us.

Only years later did it dawn on me that Dad got paid for hiring me out. Money may not have changed hands, but for my work Dad got stacks of prairie hay, which we needed because we didn't have any prairie hay on our own farm.

All summer our neighbors would process their hay: mowing it and stacking it after it was dry. All summer I helped them. I ran the stacker team, which was a pair of horses that pulled a big device used to pile the hay into stacks. We did probably three or four stacks a day, and we worked constantly during the season.

Our situation had improved enough since 1939 that Dad owned a big tractor. In 1948, he also bought a little International Harvester Farmall Model C tractor. The day *it arrived at our farm was an exciting one, but only because I didn't know I was going to end up driving it down cornrow after cornrow for hour after boring hour. At age nine or 10, I was so little I had to slide down the seat so I could reach the clutch pedal to shift gears or stop the tractor. And when I wasn't working on our farm, Dad hired me and that Model C out to replace the stacker team.*

I worked in the hay fields for two families until I was a senior in high school. By that time, the highland farmers were baling alfalfa, and they needed someone to stack bales. So I went to work for them, lifting bales that weighed 80 to 90 pounds, as much as I weighed. At the same time, I still had my chores and work to do at home.

First Things First

Many farmers depended upon "locals" like me to help them put up their hay and to do other big chores on the farm the family couldn't manage alone. The smart ones took good care of their help, because hard workers were always in demand. Smart business managers, too, take care of their employees.

Workforce Before Profit

I've always believed what's important is not the destination but the journey. If you enjoy only destinations, how many times are you going to be happy? You'd better enjoy going to school if you're going to get a Ph.D. And you'd better enjoy working with people if you're going to run a company.

Employees are a priority and, in my philosophy, workforce comes before profit. That's right, before profit. Let me state, unequivocally, humaneness, compassion, and concern for one's fellow man compel me to abide by that value. That's one reason.

A second reason, no less important, is that the people who make my company run are its most important assets. So I try to treat them that way. Where would I be without them? My future, indeed the future of everyone in the company, depends upon maintaining a work environment that nurtures their growth, protects our mutual interests, and sustains the community of people I have drawn together as the company. These people have certain expectations of their work environment. They are looking for continuity of employment, job security. They want a fair wage. They want to work in a setting that is safe and pleasant. And they think they deserve good co-workers.

Now, you may think these issues too obvious to mention. But many, many people will tolerate lower standards. They have to tolerate them if they want a job, because, although these issues are expectations, or maybe just hopes, of employees, they are not necessarily part of the mindset of the employer. To raise these expectations to reality, the employer has to think about them, articulate them, and make them components of the management philosophy, so they drive the development of policies, procedures, and programs.

Job Security

I made a conscious decision to grow our company at a pace we could sustain over the long term, so we could keep our workforce intact. I want workers who want to stay with me. Keeping the rate of employee turnover low, you avoid the costs of hiring and training new people and the period of time new employees need to gear up to full productivity.

That doesn't even take into account the psychological strain on everyone of losing familiar employees and integrating new ones into the group and the accompanying fall-off in the group's productivity. In short, even in good economic conditions, keeping your workforce intact pays off.

A Fair Wage

For many employees, discussion about work is the meat and potatoes of daily conversations. We spend about a third of our waking hours at a job and, naturally, that huge component of our lives is an ongoing topic. Just as naturally, we compare ourselves with others.

So, in a conversation about jobs, employees want to feel they are treated fairly. They want to size up their own situation against those of their friends and come out at least neck and neck, if not ahead. At a minimum, they want an equitable salary and benefits package. Some don't even have to understand their benefits fully, as long as they can say, "Oh, I have that, too."

If your company measures up to most others, you have provided your employees with the confidence they are being treated fairly. That translates into trust in you.

More Production, More Pay

Just as it's wrong for your employees to do less work than they're paid for, it's also wrong for you to expect them to work harder without additional reward. But suppose you buy a machine or a tool that helps your employees get 110 units with the same effort they once had to put forth to produce 100 units. Should you then give them a real raise to match?

Let's think about this. The employees are able to produce more without any increase in effort, because the machine itself makes that possible. With the new machine, the company brings in more money, because sales have increased with the increase in productivity. The company now is in a better position to provide inflationary wage adjustments and to offer merit increases in wages. At our company, where everyone gets a commission based on gross sales, everyone would receive a bonus.

Some of the additional income could be reinvested, so an economic cushion exists for your workforce against a future downturn in the economy.

At the same time, you, the owner, are entitled to some reward for making the payments and for shouldering the risk of owning that new machine.

A Safe and Pleasant Workplace

We spend a lot of money on clean air, clean floors, clean walls, and good equipment. We emphasize safety with well-lit work areas, a layout that is convenient and organized, a place for everything, and everything in its place. We willingly comply with all government regulations, but we go beyond the minimum requirements. In fact, our insurance company has used our shop as a safety model for other businesses.

Good Co-Workers

To have a community of good co-workers, you deliberately have to set out to compose a group of high-quality people who generally are compatible with one another. That doesn't mean everyone exchanges Christmas presents and names their children after one another. No, it means that, for the most part, they are courteous to one another, considerate, respectful, helpful – that, theoretically, they try to live by the Boy Scout code. In other words, they're good people.

Create a Team

There is no easy way to put together a good team. Like any good relationship, serendipity plays a part: You have to have the right chemistry. At the same time, assembling the right people also calls for strategy.

Start the teambuilding process with an assessment of not only your personal strengths but also, especially, your deficiencies. On the job, your weakness might be personnel matters or sales or production. Whatever it is, find people for your team who can fill in where you can't or don't want to work. I've learned that employees won't lose respect for you if you show you're only human. It's all right to admit to them you can't do something and to ask them to help you or to do it for you. It's OK to have weaknesses.

Consider, too, how employees or potential employees might need subsidizing, so you can better match your strengths with their deficiencies and vice versa. If you can figure out what your value to them is and how they can best help you, you can develop a team that benefits both of you.

When I look at an employee, I ask myself: What can I do to help him at this level of his capability, at this time in his life? Can I overcome deficiencies with education, training, experience, or human intervention? Let's say that someone isn't good at detail, but he has to attend to a certain amount of it to do his job right. I might look for another employee who enjoys doing detail work to swap around some tasks.

You're going to have a long wait if you're looking for Mr. or Ms. Perfect. But if you're looking at what resources you have to subsidize a person's deficiencies, you're on the right track for hiring people.

Two Essential Staff Positions

A bookkeeper is an indispensable position on your staff. Obviously, you can hire a service to do the work for you, and many companies do. But, somehow, somebody has to keep track of your cash flow, because you need to know where your money is coming from and where it's going.

To fill the position, you are better off hiring a professional, someone who has devoted time and training to learning how to do it right. Much is at stake in keeping your records straight. They must provide the data with which you can make vital decisions.

Don't let the bookkeeper make all the decisions about how to do the bookkeeping. Be assertive in setting up the books. Detail the kind of information you need. You will want to develop as many columns as you can define, for example, to record how you take in and spend your income. You want your records to provide you with information you can access, understand, and use.

The receptionist is another essential team member. She (yes, most receptionists are female) frees you to devote your time to managing, whether you oversee the entire company or a department, instead of attending to every phone call and every visitor. But give considerable thought to whom you hire for this position, because she also is an advertisement for your business. The receptionist is the front line of marketing – dealing with employees, customers, vendors, and the community. She gives people their first impression of your company, and you don't want her to treat them like they are interrupting her day.

In many small companies, the bookkeeper is also the receptionist. Though it may be a necessity, I think combining the two positions generally is a bad idea. In fact, "bookkeeper-receptionist" is almost an oxymoron. A professional bookkeeper, someone who has chosen the career and prepared for it, that is, tends to be a filterer of information. Bookkeepers tend to be discriminating, because they handle numbers and data, all of which have to be sorted, recorded, and tracked. Enjoying that kind of detail work, they tend to dislike interruptions.

On the other hand, a good receptionist is not a filter; she doesn't sort out people. She welcomes everybody and, especially, she enjoys people. That's what you want in this position: a goodwill ambassador. Don't confuse a receptionist with a secretary, though. A secretary is a gatekeeper, not a welcoming committee. It isn't that the person shouldn't also be pleasant; it's that the position has a different purpose, part of which is to help you manage your time.

If you must combine the positions of bookkeeper and receptionist, try at least to find a bookkeeper who has a high tolerance for people and interruptions.

Pinch Hitters

Some companies have cut staff size to the point that, if they were people, they'd be anorexic. The trend of downsizing companies to the point of gauntness for a better bottom line is a terrible short-term solution. It's all right to be slightly overstaffed. (Granted, a start-up company with only a few employees and a tight budget won't be able to afford the luxury of an additional staff person.) In fact, I advocate it, for several reasons.

One, you can better accommodate surges of work without putting a lot of stress and pressure on your people.

Two, you have greater latitude to develop and provide good training programs, which contribute to the company's long-term future. When a fire-to-put-out mentality doesn't dominate the workplace, you tend to take care of some of the practical matters of training and orientation more graciously.

Three, things that need doing but aren't yet urgent are not as likely to be put aside because nobody has time to do them until they become urgent.

Four, employees generally are happier in a relaxed and pleasant work environment than in one in crisis mode all the time. Continuous stress is unhealthy, not to mention inhumane and often unsafe. It's a surefire way to burn out your employees. You have to enjoy your work to a certain degree, and you have to be able to relax a little.

Finally, you can have people do some of the things that make the environment a little more comfortable, such as cleaning out files, getting more organized, and redesigning your immediate work area.

This concept of overstaffing is just another way of saying: Don't overwork your employees. For example, it is unfair to them to have the company so thinly staffed they can't take a vacation because the company is too busy and needs them. Time off is important for mental and physical rejuvenation.

Subordinates

Within any corporation, three groups are continuously evaluating you: your superiors, your peers, and your many subordinates. Generally, people try to impress their superiors, but many fail in getting the blessing of peers and subordinates. A good business leader attends to all three groups.

Your success depends upon your superiors' approval of you, so naturally you are concerned about what they think of you. But why care about what a peer or a subordinate thinks of you?

For one thing, as you work your way up in business, the people who work with you and for you can make your growth easy or difficult. They can work hard, cooperate with you, and support you politically, or they can make your projects a low priority, do the minimum required, and undermine your leadership. People who succeed have had subordinates who trusted them and looked out for them. In the end, people who use fear on subordinates won't succeed.

Subordinates often are violated in the workplace. They are treated with disdain, even abused, because managers think that pleasing subordinates isn't necessary. But a big part of the job of good supervisors is to protect their subordinates, to bring them up, to keep their dignity intact. So it should matter what subordinates think of you. More than that, you have an obligation to them.

Leadership

Would-be leaders can be subdivided into five categories, each one distinctive:

1. THE PERSON WANTS TO LEAD, BUT NO ONE WILL FOLLOW. Some people think that bossing others around is leadership, though they wouldn't call what they do "bossing." Even if there's only one other person nearby, they'll devote most of their time to trying to supervise that person, and they won't get anything else done.

They likely won't be good within an organization, because their bossiness, rather than being called for by a situation, is a compulsion. Consequently, it's a problem for them and for others.

2. THE PERSON WANTS TO LEAD, AND PEOPLE WILL FOLLOW. Here's a good, natural leader. This person accepts the responsibility of leadership and enjoys leading. You still have to see whether he does other things correctly, uses good judgment, makes good decisions, and so forth, but people from this group potentially make good leaders.

3. THE PERSON NEEDS TO LEAD AND, WITH TRAINING, MAY GET PEOPLE TO FOLLOW. This person has to lead because of the situation, though he may not necessarily like doing it. And if he isn't good at it, he'll require training. Because he'll only lead when he's required, he won't go as far as the person in Category Two could. He doesn't naturally enjoy leadership, so he's reluctant to respond to the challenge of leadership, unless it's necessary to reach a goal.

4. THE PERSON IS A CHARISMATIC LEADER WHO DOESN'T NECESSARILY WANT TO LEAD BUT WHOM PEOPLE WANT TO FOLLOW. This person has others in the palm of his hand, so he's capable of great good – or great evil. Because his followers naturally gravitate toward him, he may not fully appreciate the responsibility and power he has.

Those who neglect the well-being of their followers are irresponsible and, frequently, dangerous. Many obvious examples exist in the sports and entertainment industries. They exist in business, too.

5. THE PERSON IS A CHARISMATIC LEADER WHO WANTS TO LEAD AND WHOM PEOPLE BLINDLY WILL FOLLOW. This type is similar to the charismatic leader of Category Four but may be even stronger, because he relishes leadership opportunities. A Category Five leader can rally support for a cause and can accomplish wonderful things. Many politicians are obvious examples of this category. But with strength can come danger, too. For example, I'd consider Jim Jones, who led his followers to commit mass suicide, to be a Category Five leader.

If you have a charismatic individual on your staff, you have a potential leader. Upon recognizing that trait, one of the first things you should determine, before you assign serious leadership responsibility, is whether the person is of good character.

Works Well with Others

Another simple method for examining leadership concerns how comfortably people work with others. Work style, that is, whether a person enjoys working with others, can be a good indicator of the capability for leadership in the workplace. This reference categorizes work styles in three ways: independence, cooperativeness, and proximity.

Such descriptions are general, even vague, rather than absolute, because few people are absolutely one thing. And descriptions never explain the whole picture, because we humans are such complex beings. So we speak of tendencies or preferences. At least we have some kind of description that helps us explain what it is we are trying to understand.

People who prefer to work alone and who like to take sole responsibility for their work fall into the category you would expect: independent.

Few effective leaders come from this category because such people are less comfortable with others. Even when they work with others they think in terms of their own efforts. They don't enjoy taking charge of others or being in the charge of others, and they certainly don't want to be responsible for the outcome of others' efforts. When they talk about their work, they describe it in terms of their own effort, even if they are on a team project. They usually say "I" rather than "we."

People who prefer to work on a team and to share responsibility with others fall into the cooperativeness grouping. Cooperative people see things in terms of the team. They are loyal to the group of which they are a part, though not necessarily loyal to the company. "We're all in this together" is their mantra, and they want to share responsibility for everything, good and bad, with their teammates.

But that's why they don't make good leaders. They find assuming responsibility for difficult choices, well, difficult. So nobody is really in charge, or responsible for the outcome.

The work style of most people falls into the proximity, or nearness, category. People in this category like to work with or around others, and they feel responsible for the outcome of at least their own efforts. In contrast, a person in the cooperativeness grouping doesn't want individual responsibility. Out of the proximity group come our best leaders and supervisors.

If you ask them about a work experience, you'll hear them talk about other people involved in it with them, and you'll hear them describe, in some way, their desire to control the outcome. In fact, they want to be in control of their destiny, and you will hear references to that mindset.

Developing Leaders on Staff

One of the hardest tasks facing a businessperson is finding good leaders. A large part of the process is having enough experience yourself to be able to identify what you want an employee to do in a leadership role. The process of trial and error – experience – is the best way to determine leadership abilities.

I watch my people all the time, looking for promising leaders. I pick people to move forward who already are succeeding at what they're doing. And when I notice such people, I give them opportunities to do other things and see how well they do at them. I'm always determining whether they did well on a project, whether I should give them a riskier project, and whether it should be like the last one or completely different.

Remember, though, that not doing well at something doesn't mean that someone is inept, necessarily. You must try to determine why that person failed. Was it because he didn't have enough information? Was it because unforeseen circumstances worked against him? Was it because he just was unwilling to put forth enough effort? You look for problems he didn't recognize, problems for which he could have changed the outcome by altering his input.

A Fate Worse than Failure

Just as you have to look at why a good leader fails, you have to consider whether you may have on your hands a poor leader who just happened to be in the right place at the right time for a promotion. Many people are snookered by individuals who succeed not because of themselves but in spite of themselves. And the reason people are snookered is they don't evaluate the situations in which those individuals succeeded. The most obvious and egregious examples occur in politics – but I'll stick to my own realm.

It happens not infrequently among job applicants, for example. I am skeptical of résumés that say: "I saved the company $250,000, and I cut 7,000 worker-hours on my project." I know that, in most companies, it was a team that brought about the success. The bragging individual just happened to be involved in the project. That's an obvious example of false leadership, and if you don't scrutinize the circumstances, you may find yourself seriously disappointed by the person's real capabilities.

Likewise, when you observe how your own employees succeed or fail at a leadership task, take into account the environment in which they worked. How much did they affect it? Did they get others to cooperate with them? Was the economy one that helped them succeed, or did they succeed in spite of it? Did they put a lot of creativity into the project? Could anyone have been successful with that project at that particular time?

Do You Really Need a Leader?

For many supervisory settings in business, though, you don't necessarily need a leader. And often, you can delegate projects successfully even to people who have no desire to lead, simply by passing along to them a procedure you developed.

My process was simple: Create a procedure, test it, try it out over several cycles, and, when I'm sure it works, teach it to somebody else. Bookkeeping is an example. Some others are costing a job, going through accounts payable, and paying the checks. When I was starting my business, I did all those tasks myself first. Then I taught someone else to do them the way I wanted them done. While the person was learning a procedure, I would have him bring the work to me to double-check and approve.

We now have tasks that are four developmental generations or more from when I designed them. They're still being done in pretty much the way I designed them, just improved.

Limits of Leadership

Your ability to lead depends upon how well your supervisors carry out the responsibilities you delegate to them. But remember, there are practical limits as well as personal limits to each person's capacity. Some studies indicate a supervisor loses effectiveness when he is directly responsible for more than about 10 people. Keep that number in mind as you organize and expand your workforce. Help your supervisors perform to the best of their ability by keeping their workload within reasonable parameters. In turn, their success will enhance your leadership.

Troublesome Employees

You should be dismayed when you begin hearing the wrong questions and the wrong complaints from an employee. He's signaling that he isn't developing along lines that are going to be helpful to the corporation or to your other employees. I once had a welder who wanted every step of a job – all the procedures – laid out for him. It was an impossible task, because every project we fabricate is different. Each one consists of a series of choices.

This welder was in the wrong work environment for his personality; he was a procedural person in an options job. As a result, he was nervous and unsettled. We encouraged him to find a job in an environment appropriate for him, one with more repetitive tasks and specific procedures to follow.

The Free Spirit

A person with nothing to lose is going to be a source of problems. He will take unnecessary risks. He won't care much about how his behavior affects those around him. And at the first sign of difficulty, he'll leave.

On the other hand, a person who has some personal responsibilities and obligations, even if they consist of just rent and a car payment, has something at stake. He is more likely to think about consequences if he has something to lose, so an employment relationship with that person is possible.

You can't ask direct questions about these issues, but you can glean information from what a prospective employee says.

Fat Cats

A fat cat is someone whose income has exceeded his output. Let's say the company expects its employees to produce 100 units of work a day, for which each will be paid $100 a day. A new employee might be able to do only 80 units of work, for which he is paid $80 a day. Then he improves to 90 units and gets a raise to $90. Finally, after training and hard work, he is up to speed. He can produce 100 units of work, for which he earns $100 a day. He has reached his goal. Whew!

But if he slacks off to 90 units, or even 80, while he's getting (we can't say "earning") $100 a day, he becomes a fat cat, a parasite in your business who is getting more than he is giving. Fat cats are inflationary in the economics of a company. If you are paying $100 for 100 units of work ($1 per unit), an employee who is producing only 90 units actually is costing you just over $1.11 per unit.

In other words, you have a rate of inflation of 11 percent on that employee's productivity. Put another way, if you permit that employee to slack off to 90 units, you have given him a "raise" of 11 percent — generous of you! But better for you to remind him that he has to put out 100 units for the 100-unit pay.

Outgo Problems

Some employees have an unrealistic view of the marketplace. They expect to earn what they want to earn, without regard for whether the marketplace pays that much for their set of skills. They blame the employer for not paying them enough.

Other employees don't have an income problem; they have an outgo problem, because they spend beyond their means, even though they earn a good wage. A person who doesn't live within his income (assuming a living wage) will be a continuous source of frustration. Many times, his solution to his outgo problem is to complain to his employer that he isn't making enough. "I can't live on what I'm making," he'll say. I pose the question: "What are you personally going to do to be worth more?"

Over the years, when employees have complained about wages, the first thing I do is look at the marketplace. I like the company to be in the upper quartile in the community for wages paid for a particular job. Second, I review how much the employee loses by being tardy, taking excessive time off, or not working overtime when asked.

One of my employees in the early 1970s always was having money problems. He actually was reducing his income by an average of $600 a year because he was frequently late, took excessive time off, and wouldn't work overtime. In 1970 dollars, that's a lot of money. He couldn't see that it was within his power and, certainly, it was his responsibility to get that $600.

As he described his situation at home, I could see why he'd have to borrow change on Monday mornings just to get a candy bar. He would have his family bring him to work, then bring him lunch, then pick him up. That's three round trips a day, a lot of gas. No one would car-pool with him because he was so frequently late and because he was always mooching. So I didn't take seriously his complaints about his welfare or quality of life. He could have solved his money problems with the help of his family and a little self-discipline.

Mind Your Business

People seem to have a vision of what a manager should be and do. Don't fall into the trap of thinking a president or a manager should do only certain things. In companies really making money, you will see owners or presidents or managers doing all sorts of things just to keep workers busy. Ego is not an issue. In fact, the smart leader sees his job as keeping workers' "cups" full and pitching in for the overflow.

You can measure how fast your business is growing by how quickly your own cup overflows. My process of growth was to fill every day with at least 12 hours of work and, when it grew longer than 12 hours, to delegate some of the tasks to other people. It also was a measure of when I should consider hiring more people.

Manager as Mom or Dad – Bad

An outsider might observe how closely the role of manager resembles that of parent. Managers have responsibility for other people, their subordinates. They know more (about the company). They understand the big picture better than subordinates do. In addition, their subordinates are beholden to them for many things, including approval, somewhat as kids are to parents.

But don't let that superficial observation dupe you into assuming a parental role with your workers, no matter how immature their behavior or how great the difference between your ages. Many people didn't get along well with their parents. If you play mommy or daddy in the workplace, you're going to struggle with many of your employees. Just like they resisted their parents' control, they're going to resist yours. They're going to question your authority. They're going to challenge you.

Assuming a parental role in the workplace is subsidizing gone astray. Mothering a competent employee will make that employee angry, and mothering an incompetent one will make everyone else in the department angry. Co-workers understand when a new employee who is inexperienced needs special attention.

But when a person who has been there long enough to be trained and to have the necessary experience still needs extra attention, that person is not measuring up and should be removed from the group. Instead, the mothering supervisor, rather than do the right thing, will protect the substandard employee, at the expense of all the others.

Give employees reasonable opportunities to grow into their duties, but make them responsible for their own behavior. If they're frequently late to work, for example, hold them accountable. A hundred excuses for tardiness by a lackadaisical worker don't compensate for the extra effort the rest of the group has to make.

Say It with Sugar

We humans seem to resist being commanded. For one thing, it expresses an attempt to control us. It implies someone is trying to infringe on our independence. It perhaps even smacks of an expectation of servitude. In some instances, such as the military, we tolerate it, but employees, in general, expect to be treated a bit more appreciatively.

A supervisor who gives directions to subordinates as commands rather than requests is setting himself up for a staff of resentful employees, and the chips on their shoulders could be very difficult to knock off. "Please" and "Thank you" go a long way in smoothing the rough edges of a directive.

Many situations call for another part to the directive: an explanation of why it's needed. If you tell somebody why you want that person to do something, you're changing the situation from a simple request into an educational moment.

Think of the difference between "Turn the sheet of aluminum around" and "If you turn the sheet of aluminum this way, the next worker won't cut his hands when he picks it up." It's not only "nice" to explain such things to your workers, it's obligatory. Part of the manager's job is to educate subordinates, so it's up to you to tell them what they don't grasp for themselves.

When management doesn't take the time to explain an issue, it's usually for one of two reasons. One, supervisors haven't figured out what's really going on; they haven't sat down and thought and talked about it. Set aside some time occasionally just to sit down with your supervisors and talk about what's happening, about trends, about the environment both inside and outside the company, about the future.

It may feel like just shooting the bull, but if it's directed toward issues, however general, that relate to the business, it can provide an opportunity for them to learn from your experience, to reflect on what they observe in their own situation, and to mature in their role as managers.

The second reason managers don't explain an issue is that they sometimes just tend to keep things to themselves. They often don't understand that another person might need more information for a task than they do. Managers should allow for questions and give the person asking as much information as practical, including written material.

Give Praise and Credit in Every Direction

Think of your position in the company as the center of a big plus sign. There are people above you, people below you, and people on either side of you. The plus sign stands for your relationship with those around you. Because of that relationship, you owe them praise when they do a good job. There's no need to be lavish about it, but do be sincere and, especially, prompt.

Keep in mind some people accept praise easily and others don't. Most people accept praise from someone they respect and, generally, politics more or less forces your subordinates to respect your position, whether or not they otherwise would respect you. So they likely will accept – in fact, expect – praise from you. Equally important, though, is to show appreciation to people who are above you and to peers around you.

Avoid Cookie-Cutter Criticism

People take criticism more easily from someone who also compliments them occasionally, but I don't buy into the theory that you should compliment a person before you criticize him. Cookie-cutter management techniques come across as phony. You cannot apply a formula to such decisions.

They depend, rather, on appropriateness and timeliness. Is this the right time, the right way to do it for this person? When an employee on a shearing machine is using the machine incorrectly, he should be criticized constructively right then, before he cuts off a hand or damages the machine. Never mind trying to think of a compliment first. You can make your remark politely, of course. Criticism, after all, doesn't require being mean.

You have an obligation to correct your subordinates, graciously, of course, when they didn't do something the way you want it done. That can be difficult. I am still learning.

Some Important Personnel Policies

If you have even one employee, you need a personnel policy. It may be formal or informal, written or spoken, but it's necessary. You need some means of telling your workers what you will do for them, what you expect from them, and what you won't tolerate. Indeed, you have the responsibility to give them that information, so everybody clearly understands the standards. A company with several employees should have a written personnel policy handbook, one reviewed and approved by legal counsel familiar with employment issues.

Sexual Harassment

In an effort to create and maintain an equitable workplace, the federal government has tried to legislate behavior, seemingly, to the nth degree. Even words or gestures that otherwise might indicate appreciation or concern are suspect in our wary minds. In many ways, we are overly alert for the slightest hint of disrespect or mistreatment.

Yet, the rules did evolve from the need to delineate for the ill-bred, chauvinistic, and predatory types among us what behavior is appropriate or not appropriate among workers, so no one is abused and no one takes advantage of anyone.

Government regulations set a standard regarding control of sexual harassment in the workplace. Spell out clearly in your employee handbook the rules concerning sexual harassment, and tolerate no abuse of them. Serious violation of those rules should be grounds for immediate dismissal.

It should go without saying that hanging "girlie" pictures on the walls is inappropriate; yet, a tour of many shops, staffed mostly by men, gives one quite an eyeful. How can an owner who allows the display of offensive materials in the workplace say with a straight face the company promotes respect for men and women alike?

Surely, no woman would believe or accept such a statement. Set the rules so you have a setting in which any one of your customers or employees – male or female – can go anywhere in the company without being distressed by pornographic or other offensive materials.

Booze at Company Parties

Drunken employees at a company Christmas party may seem funny enough in a TV sitcom, but they are no laughing matter for the conscientious manager. Allowing liquor at company parties, let alone providing it, is a terrific responsibility. If you serve booze at a company gathering and one of your guests, while driving home, runs into somebody, you probably are going to be in court.

For that matter, if a drunken employee accosts another employee at the party, you probably are going to be in court. All kinds of scary scenarios come to mind when you look at the issue with the healthy paranoia I recommend.

At the same time, people in social settings do like to relax with a drink and there must be a happy medium between debauchery and teetotalism. At our company, we have been willing to accept the responsibility for serving liquor, and we believe we have taken a reasonable approach to the situation. Our company parties are offsite, and we let caterers assume the liability of physically serving the liquor. We limit to two drinks the amount of free liquor we serve, and we limit the length of time in which we serve it. Happy hour is just that: an hour.

In addition, it is a good idea to serve food with liquor and to make soft drinks available. And, of course, you should verify that the employees served are old enough to drink legally.

Safety

The work we do in our shop is dangerous. We operate machines that shear and stamp and weld metal. We use acids. We use saws. We drive forklifts and trucks. We lift and carry all kinds of stuff. We operate heavy tools and move heavy pieces of metal from place to place. We climb around on the machines we build.

Despite that, we have an excellent safety record, which merits a deduction on our insurance premium. In fact, our casualty-insurance carrier has visited our plant to see which of our practices might be transferable to other customers in the same industry who are having accidents.

Even before the regulations that mandate a safety committee, we made safety an ingrained part of our culture. Everybody is a safety watchdog. We teach our employees that safety comes before anything else, and we don't allow any infraction of safety rules to go by without comment and correction.

One of our safety practices is to ensure employees are properly trained on any machine they operate, so we require that employees have an "operator's license" for each machine they use and that they periodically renew that license. Nobody is allowed to operate a machine on which he is not current on safety and operational training.

In addition, we make available all the materials and manuals concerning the operation, maintenance, and safe handling of the equipment, and we require that, every so often, the employees sit down and read those books. Once an employee signs off on that requirement, we renew his license to operate each machine he studied.

In our business at least, taking a vacation is also a matter of safety. A tired or overworked employee can be a dangerous one. Besides, everybody needs a break occasionally. We encourage family vacations and getaways by making available to our employees camping directories for the state park system. We also provide state tourism packets and maps of Nebraska and Iowa (we're near the state border).

Chapter 7
Taking Care of Employees

W hen I was little, our dog, Queenie, had puppies, but my older brother, Nelson, got first pick, and he picked the one I liked best: a brown, happy ball of fur. We gave the rest away. All farms had dogs for protection against predators (predators that like chickens). It wasn't hard to get rid of a litter of pups.

Nelson was gone a lot, so Brownie slowly became my dog. If Brownie had been a person, he'd have been a genius. There wasn't anything he couldn't figure out, it seemed. He was part border collie, so handling cattle came naturally to him, and he was a constant help to me when I worked the cattle.

Milking the cows always started with getting them to the milk barn. In the cool months, when the grass wasn't growing very fast, they would stay closer to the barn in the morning and evening, because they looked forward to the treats they would get when we'd let them into the milk parlor.

But in the summer, when the grasses were juicy and rich, the cows would go way off down the pasture, and I would have to go get them with a horse, or walk down, and round them up and herd them to the farmstead.

Brownie learned to herd the cows for me. All I would have to say was, "Go get 'em, Brownie!" and he'd take off running. Cows with bags full of milk don't like to be hurried, and Brownie was smart enough not to hurry them. At the same time, he was all business, and he would nip any who tried to linger for another bite of grass. For years this was the ceremony morning and night, until Brownie died.

Surprisingly, even long after he was gone, I could go out to the edge of the pasture and yell "Go get 'em, Brownie!" and the cows would slowly turn and come to the barn.

Before You Hire

Dogs have introductions down to the basics: they sniff tails. It's simple, quick, and straightforward; the results are unambiguous. Hiring employees should be so easy. Introducing a new employee into the "pack" of a work group is one of the most important aspects of managing a business. It has to be taken seriously.

Describe the Job

Success of the hiring process depends upon an important preliminary: an accurate job description. First, how can you know the kind of employee you really need if you don't know what the job really entails? Just calling the position "store clerk" isn't enough. Is the position part time or full time? Is it temporary? Is the person to open or close the store? Staff the store alone? Supervise others? Handle cash transactions? Stock shelves? Place orders? Take inventory? Make bank deposits? Assess quality of incoming stock? The list continues, but you get the point.

Second, if you don't have an accurate job description, how can you properly evaluate the employee's performance? The person won't know what you really want if you don't define it clearly enough that you both know what "doing a good job" means. A good job description is fundamental to a good relationship with your employees.

So scrutinize the position you want to fill. Identify the duties and responsibilities it really comprises. Look at the qualifications, experience, and physical requirements the position actually requires of the worker. Consider the job with personality and temperament in mind.

For example, does the job require attention to detail, as bookkeeping does? Is it a procedural job with the same duties each day? Does it require the worker to come up with many options?

You don't have to do all this analysis yourself. Talk to people in the department where the job is available. Especially if the job is unusual, talk with others who worked or will work with the employee in that position.

Find out what the employee who last had the job actually did. If the person failed, ask other workers why they think that happened. It's an important question – often you will hear an answer you hadn't considered. Chances are, if you don't analyze why an employee failed, you will repeat a hiring mistake.

Finally, compare the position with similar positions in other companies (another good reason to network). Your careful analysis will pay off in a closer fit between worker and work. That's a huge move toward reducing employee turnover.

Cast the Right Bait

Choosing the right employee from a pool of applicants is no easy task. In fact, if none of the applicants looks right, you may have attracted the wrong pool of applicants. With the right kind of ad, you can improve your selection by appealing to the most fitting applicants in the first place. The suitability of the people who respond will depend upon how well you understand what kind of personality traits the job requires. By using words addressing the traits you seek, you can create an ad that raises the caliber of your whole pool of applicants.

When I began writing employment ads, I thought of my company as dynamic and growing. I portrayed it that way. The words I used attracted people who liked change and thought in short time spans.

But this kind of employee wasn't right for our shop, and I knew it, even though at the time I couldn't articulate the problem.

I was focused on describing the company rather than the kind of employee I wanted. Our company was dynamic and growing, yes, but I wanted employees looking for a stable environment, people who liked a sense of continuity and who had an eye for the long term. I wanted employees who would be with me five years later.

Once I realized my ads were attracting the opposite kind of person, I changed my focus to the company's reputation as a long-established, respected institution. The strategy helped. I attracted applicants who would fit into the stable community I was building, and from this filtered group of potential employees, I could choose the best.

A job ad should include some basic elements. One, read the job description, and consider the personality requirements of the position; then list the required education and experience. Two, include the five most important traits necessary for success in the job, such as: "must enjoy working with people" or "must be self-starter" or "attention to detail required." Three, mention potential "deal breakers." Don't waste time interviewing applicants who wouldn't even have applied had they known beforehand that the job entails, say, a lot of travel, odd working hours, or unusual working conditions.

Is the Applicant in the Right Field?

Don't assume an applicant is a good fit for a job just because he has the skills and has a degree after his name. Many an employee is hired for such reasons or because the employee comes across well in an interview. None of those reasons is wrong, but they don't go far enough. It is more important to select an employee by matching, as closely as possible, the characteristics of the individual to the personality requirements of the company and the job.

Hire for Good

How do you view the hiring process? Is it a serendipitous event? An inconvenience? An interruption of your normal business activities? Or is it a polished procedure? An opportunity? An important part of your workforce-improvement program? You know by now how I would answer those questions.

Enhance Your Team

Above all, hiring is not a power issue. The process should be a thoughtful and soul-searching one. Your overriding determination should be: Will hiring this person move the quality of my workforce up, down, or sideways? Don't just try to fill job slots. At our company, we would rather leave a position open if we can't find a person of high enough personal quality, no matter what his qualifications.

On the other hand, if an outstanding applicant walks in, we might hire the person and find something for the individual to do, even though we don't have an immediate opening. It's a great opportunity to expand the capability of the workforce, one of a manager's most important jobs, and if you don't snap up extraordinary people when they come along, you probably won't get a second chance when you really need them.

The interim financial bottom line isn't as important as getting a good person on your team, getting him trained, and getting him up to speed so you'll be ready when you do need him. In other words, you're increasing capacity. I acknowledge this wasn't possible when we had only 10 employees. However, it gets easier to do as the company grows and the pool of financial resources deepens.

Find the Diamonds

If you want the best person you can get, look at character and mental abilities, aptitudes as well as skills. Work history is important. Knowing how frequently an applicant changes jobs will give you a good indication of whether you can count on him for the long term or will have to replace him in the near future.

We also look at whether a potential employee is going to fit into our particular environment. Should that person be at a big company or a small one? Is he going to be able to interact with the people in our organization? A "no" doesn't mean the candidate is a bad person; it just means the fit doesn't feel right.

My No. 1 job as a manager is to protect my work community, so it's part of my job to be sure any new employee is going to be compatible with the rest of the employees. People shouldn't have to work with someone who's rude and offensive.

If you hire a person who, because of being disruptive, brings down by even 5 percent the productivity of 10 people with whom he works closely, look at what you've lost, besides putting people through misery. Especially, I look for ways potential employees stand out from the pack. Early on I learned to look first for people making an extra effort. Then I figure out whether it's part of the person's real character or whether he's just trying to make a temporary impression.

That kind of insight has helped me place at the head of my departments outstanding people who are contributors, always working. When a job needs to be done, they do it, regardless of whether anyone recognizes their effort. Going the extra mile is part of their substance.

Expectations vs. Reality

Another issue I consider in a job interview is whether a person's expectations of achievement are realistic and appropriate for his set of attributes, skills, education, and experience. I have in mind a sort of expectation-realization graph: Down the left side is a measure of achievement, usually in income; across the bottom is a time line. Ideally, the chart that emerges when you plot a person's expectations for future success reflects his accurate estimation of his own unique combination of elements.

But as you might expect, sometimes the individual's notions of his possibilities are overrated. If he has an education that will get him a job paying $20,000 a year, but he expects to be making $50,000 in just a few years, I have to ask, at least to myself: What is going to intercede in his life that will make that expectation come true? How much value is going to be added through experience at our company? Is he planning to get more education that later might justify an income at that level?

In other words, does he have a strategy for growth, or does he just naively expect that his charm and good looks are going to loosen the company purse strings? If it turns out to be the latter, I know he will not be a good employee for us, because he will never be realistic.

The Hiring Process

We look everywhere for potential employees. People walk in and ask for a job. We get referrals. We run newspaper ads. We hire employees from companies that go out of business or downsize. But all our applicants, no matter the source, go through the same multiple-step, multiple-person hiring process.

You simply must have a procedure that applies equally to all applicants, one that excludes irrelevant elements and impulsive responses. Hiring a person simply for looks, for example, is foolish. We have created a procedure that works for us, one that abides by government guidelines and that our labor attorney has approved.

Multiple Steps

Our potential employees fill out an application form. With the application, we give them a list of items we know are potential deal breakers. For example, we require a drug test and don't allow smoking except in designated areas. Some candidates leave the application on the counter and walk out when they read the list. By letting applicants know up front, we don't waste the interview process on someone already dissatisfied because of those issues.

After this initial screening, the applicant is interviewed by someone from our human resource department. We get to know him a little better, and we make sure he gets to know us.

We look at whether an applicant's set of assets fits our needs. If the person has greater skills than the job requires, but they're skills we will need later, we might be willing to hire the applicant and pay a higher salary for those additional skills. But if the applicant is overqualified for the position we need to fill and we won't need his additional talents, we say so. Hiring an overqualified person seldom does anyone any good. He simply will get bored with the job and look for opportunity elsewhere. We know more about the company's current needs and future needs than does the applicant. It is our responsibility to evaluate compatibility.

From this point, if the applicant still seems to be a legitimate candidate, we send him on to interview with a committee of the people under whom he's going to work. This step is important. Putting into a work group someone its supervisors haven't met is a bad practice; it's unfair to everyone. Essentially, the committee interview is an opportunity to get acquainted. The committee decides if the individual is likely to fit into the company in general and into the department specifically.

We compare potential employees not only with the other applicants but also with the people who have done the job in the past. Having a group of foremen who are long-term employees gives us a good perspective. Someone might say: "Remember the problem we had with So-and-So. He wasn't happy here because of this, and I think we're getting right back into the same situation."

Obviously, we don't want to hire someone for an environment unsuitable for him because, if he's unhappy, he'll make others around him unhappy.

If the supervisors give an applicant a "thumbs up," then we have him read our handbook, which describes the history of the company and such details as personnel policies and the components of our benefits program and our pay system.

We want our employees to have a context for the work they do and to know as much about our employee programs as they can. We expect the applicant to read the handbook right there in the office for as long as it takes. We even provide a notepad and encourage the person to write down questions for discussion later.

Next, the applicant takes a skill test, if the position requires it. The department heads who administer the skill test discuss the results, consider the whole situation, and rank the candidates who get this far.

Does it seem odd to wait this far into the process to see how good an applicant's skills are? The set of skills is only a portion of the applicant's assets. I'd rather have an employee with a lesser set of skills who has a good work ethic, someone who tries hard, someone who's conscientious, someone who works well with others than somebody with a high set of skills who can't talk to co-workers politely or who argues with the foreman or who often complains or who is always questioning what he's supposed to be doing.

We offer the job to the top applicant. We may not always get the first person on the list; we may go down to the third or fourth person. But all applicants on the list – and only those on the list – are eligible. If we can't get any of those applicants, we don't continue on to those who didn't qualify. We just say no and start the process over. But we make that decision together, and we do it systematically.

Anatomy of the Interview

Before you interview applicants, carefully review the job description and rank the value of the requirements. For simpler jobs, two categories may be sufficient: the applicant either can do the job or can't. For many jobs, though, some requirements are more important than others and deserve more weight.

For each requirement the applicant meets, points go into the "can do" column. At the end of the interview, I total the scores and rank the applicants, offering the job to the applicant with the most points in the "can do" column.

Make a list of questions and ask them of every candidate. This gives you a fairer comparison on which to base your hiring decision. Granted, no two interviews will be exactly alike, but you'll be closer to an objective analysis. Give yourself time between interviews to carefully review the information you've collected. You don't want the interviews to homogenize or run together in your mind.

Job interviews will go more smoothly if you stick to a simple regimen. Limit the initial interview to one hour, of which you spend about 45 minutes determining whether the person can do the job and 10 minutes answering the applicant's questions, interspersed with five minutes of relaxing chitchat. If you think the person is a strong candidate, schedule a second interview and, if necessary, subsequent ones.

Spend that 45 minutes listening as much as possible. Your task is to match the job requirements with what the applicant offers. The job description is your guide, and both you and the applicant should have a copy of it.

Any point at which the demands of the job and the applicant's package of talents don't overlap indicates a need for subsidy. The applicant may have to have additional training or field experience or practice using office equipment. No one will be a perfect fit, but the amount of subsidy required is an important consideration, because it will come out of supervisory time.

The 10-minute question period is important. The applicant's questions give you additional opportunities to see how the person thinks. Was the subject covered in the interview? Should it have been covered? Is it important?

We note how curious an applicant is about us. Making a decision to go to work for an employer is as big as the employer's decision to hire an individual. Applicants who don't take the situation seriously enough to find out more about the company and to consider whether it fits with their expectations may be making a frivolous decision. The subsequent decision, when the applicant is your employee, to go elsewhere for another five cents an hour will be just as poorly considered.

The interview process is fraught with pitfalls. A poorly defined job description will get you off to a bad start. Cutting off an applicant's response is another problem. Interrupting the applicant's answers interrupts your opportunity to learn more about the person.

An even worse mistake is selling the applicant on the company or the job. Interviewers often interject their own attitude about the company, turning the interview away from learning about the applicant.

If you're talking, you're disclosing, and you're skewing the interview, because the applicant will try to respond to what you like or don't like.

And if you start explaining benefits, you are eliminating the opportunity to hear the applicant's questions. Any information you give is that much the applicant won't ask about. Instead, find out what the applicant believes is important.

Ask questions, then be quiet until the applicant has finished answering. Wait until the last part of the interview to provide information, in response to the applicant's inquiries.

A Good Start

One of the most stressful days in a person's life is the first day on a new job. A new employee is grateful when you give him a gracious, empathetic welcome. We assign each new employee to a "buddy," who is available to answer the new employee's questions and to introduce him to co-workers.

We spend quite a bit of time reviewing the handbook – what's expected of the employee and what's expected of others. In addition to the personnel handbook, a formal orientation program that routinely covers the basics helps to ensure we don't overlook something important.

Each company's list will be different, and it should include much more than showing the person where the break room, the restrooms, and the fire exits are and what to do in case of a tornado. It is vital in helping a new employee fit in and feel welcome. I believe if an employee's first day is a good one, he is more likely to keep a good attitude.

Take Training Seriously

Training often is a failure point. Employees improperly trained experience frustration on the job, develop a poor attitude, and cost the company because of errors and early resignation. Carefully train a new employee for his new position.

First, make sure your training staff is adequate for that important task.

Second, teach the employee in the modality in which he learns best. The four learning modalities are: see, hear, read, and do. Eighty percent of us learn best by watching, but others learn best by hearing or reading, or by doing something themselves.

Talk to the employee about how he likes to learn. He may not be aware of his preference, though, so I suggest you cover all the modalities in the training process. Once you notice he's getting bored with one approach, go to the next. I show him so he can see. I tell him how to do the job, so he can hear. I give him material to take home and review so he can read about it. Then I go over the job with him as he performs it.

Settling In

I cringe when I hear of a company whose training program is basically sink or swim. That's a cold, unkind way to induct a new employee, guaranteed to increase his stress level. And to what end?

We try to put a new employee to work on something with which he's familiar and on which he can be trained in a few minutes. Accomplishing an easy task at first builds confidence, and it helps a new worker develop a positive frame of mind about his job, which certainly makes the job of a manager easier.

If a worker is going to run a machine, we might start him out as a helper to someone who's already knowledgeable about it. Some employees are better teachers than others, so be careful about choosing the employee to whom you assign someone for orientation.

We formally evaluate new employees twice during their first year with us. As they learn and grow into their job, it is important they get adequate feedback so they understand clearly what they are to do and where they need to improve. It is not fair to terminate someone for doing a bad job if you haven't taught him well.

Blips in the Process

Hiring isn't a perfect process, of course. Even with every effort to follow the guidelines, we still make mistakes. At the extreme, mistakes can be rectified by the termination process, another equally arduous and systematic procedure. But let me caution you about some scenarios, in the hope of helping you avoid having to make that gut-wrenching decision.

Cash Only

All employees work for money. That's a given, but if money is the only consideration they have, consider it a yellow flag. As you've already read, some employees decide what they should be paid by looking at what they need or want rather than what the market will pay for their set of skills.

If an applicant tells you the reason he wants a job with you is to earn money, rather than because of interesting projects, gaining experience, a nice work environment, quality fellow workers, or personal growth, basically he's telling you he'll likely always take the highest offer – whenever it comes along.

Hire My Friend

If an employee says, "I have this friend who's looking for a job, and he's really good," take care. Often, though not always, when you ask that employee about his friend's work qualifications, you will find he knows next to nothing about them. He likes this person because they play canasta or go bowling together.

Don't blindly accept the hiring recommendations of employees. Put their suggested candidates through the same rigorous hiring process through which you put every other applicant.

In fact, think twice if an employee wants you to hire a friend, and never hire an employee's relative. If one leaves, you might lose the other as well. Once, when I terminated one of two brothers who worked for me, the other one criticized me for it and quit. Yet, when the second one had an opportunity to hire his brother, he didn't. I guess he knew him well enough after all.

Hiring someone who wasn't screened properly creates problems of all kinds. He might work for a week, then say, "This isn't for me."

Even so, despite all our efforts to prevent it with proper procedures, that still happens to us occasionally.

Hiring Family Members

If you hire your family members, bend over backward to make sure you are fair to your other employees. It's a touchy situation. The family member has to be better than the other employees to be perceived by them as good enough. And when you promote a family member over other employees, he has to excel beyond what you would expect of them, and what they themselves would expect to achieve, if they are to accept his promotion.

Salary

No matter what you pay employees, whether part time or full time, follow the rules. Don't deal in cash so you can fudge on taxes. Don't call employees "consultants" to avoid paying social security and other salary-related taxes. If you get caught, you are in big trouble. Even if you don't get caught, you still are cheating.

What's more, you are undermining your own authority and your employees' respect for you by demonstrating you think it's all right to break the rules. How can you then expect your workers not to break company rules? Always be a good example.

Keep Salaries in Line

We keep an eye on what the market is paying in salary and benefits to people with the same skills our employees have. One way we do that is by paying close attention during job interviews to what applicants say about the salary, benefits, and incentives they had at their last job. We try to stay in the upper quartile of the community.

We also consider the worth of each employee in terms of the group. Believing each employee has an intrinsic value to the group, we look at that value. That is, which employees have skills hard to find or train for, or values or attributes, other than what are called for in their job description, that make them unusually important to the company?

Your Workers' Finances Affect Your Company

Your workers' financial condition and solvency are important to your company's financial resiliency. If a high percent of your workforce lives on credit or does not have a strategy for economic downturns, the precarious financial position of the overall group will reduce your company's economic safety cushion. If employees have borrowed and spent and now look ahead to years of payments on top of their normal expenditures, they will not be able to afford an economic setback of any kind.

As a group, they can exert pressure on management to at least preserve their economic situation. They can force you to take into account their inability to tolerate cost-cutting measures that might crimp their income even temporarily. Put simply, they can limit your choice of options. Those options could be critical to protecting or preserving your company – the company that provided them jobs in the first place.

On the other hand, if you have a group of people who can tolerate outside economic pressure because they practice good, fiscally conservative habits, you have a wider range of options and a greater safety cushion.

Wise spending helps employees avoid financial difficulty and contributes to their economic peace of mind. That financial security goes a long way toward satisfaction with their job. One of the reasons our company retains employees is that the structure of our salary program makes spending money wisely more convenient for them.

Our Salary Program

We created our salary program with a financial timeline in mind, one that considers a general pattern of income and outgo. Here's what I mean.

In the short term, a week to a month, we all have such bills as rent or mortgage payments, groceries, utilities, credit-card charges, gas, and other miscellaneous expenses – some discretionary – associated with daily life. One has to think only a month ahead to plan for those costs.

The intermediate term, which I consider a month to about six months, might include such bills as insurance premiums and perhaps the cost of longer-life items – a new suit, tools, a washing machine – things not consumed within 30 days, things for which we have to save.

The long term, more than six months, would include much costlier items that must be planned and saved for: vacation or college education, for example.

Hence, our employees receive a weekly paycheck, a monthly bonus based on the month's sales, and a yearly bonus. They also participate in a program of deferred compensation.

The weekly paycheck is dependable. We intend it to cover those regular bills people generally incur monthly. The monthly bonus check, part of the sales commission we pay each hourly employee as an incentive, is like a buffer. It can be set aside for unfortunate surprises or a budget for large purchases, such as a new washer or dryer.

The year-end check, the other portion of the sales-commission incentive, is another buffer. Some people use it for Christmas, for which they otherwise might borrow and incur debt. Others might use it to pay off a short-term loan or to set aside as additional savings.

The pressure on people to overspend for Christmas and for vacation can be a problem for an employer. In January and February, when Christmas bills pile up, some workers become disgruntled about their salaries. But by structuring the incentive program for a check at the end of the year, I "redeemed" myself, because employees have cash to spend when they need it. The lump sum is easier to save, too, if they prefer to apply it toward a big vacation.

Lastly, our deferred-compensation program helps employees plan for that time that seems always to be beyond the horizon. Left to our own devices, most of us don't think that far ahead. More urgent wants and needs take precedence over hazy eventuality.

Our workforce is more stable because of our built-in budgeting system. Without being intrusive or nosy, our salary structure is a good way to help employees manage their money. We do it for the sake of the company, as well as for them.

Incentives

Whereas benefits are part of the employment package, incentives, whether year-end bonuses or some other form of reward, are usually related to programs designed to increase performance. They may be temporary or long term, although I am not sure long-term incentive programs work as well as they once did. Today, people seem less inspired by them. Perhaps it's because the workforce is more mobile and less loyal to a company, in many cases justifiably so.

Regardless, the first rule to remember about incentives is that, sooner or later, employees come to consider them benefits. That is, people come to feel entitled to them. Unless you make clear the program is temporary, you remove it at your peril.

For example, if you plan an incentive for being on time or for not missing work and it is part of a temporary program, you'd better inform people that it's temporary right away, or you will be remembered for having taken away things when you end it. However generous the program, you won't be remembered for giving, and you will have hurt morale. That said, incentives are useful, provided you design them carefully.

The Carrot and the Stick

Establish the purpose of the incentive program, then design the program as purely as you can, so it relates only to the behavior you're trying to address and doesn't affect other aspects of the business. Consider the size of the "carrot" and the length of the "stick." Is a small carrot on such a long stick that there's no enthusiasm for achievement?

Employees quickly figure out if goals are unrealistic. Be sure goals are reasonably attainable. Weigh the design of the program. Should it have a big carrot on a long stick, or a little carrot on a short stick? The two types aren't the same. In addition, look carefully for all the ways in which the program could be manipulated.

Apply Incentives to All Employees

Sometimes managers tie an incentive to too many issues or to issues relevant only to some employees. For instance, some companies reward the salespeople with commissions and treat the rest of the staff like a support system for them. Oh, management might get a bonus if the company does well, but everybody else is taken for granted.

What happens to the company, then, if an overzealous sales force, driven by commissions, makes promises the production staff can't keep? What happens to the company if the sales force sells the services, but the workers who perform them do a bad job? The sales force has gotten its reward, yet the company still has difficulty delivering a satisfactory product.

Better to develop an incentive program that accounts for the effort of every employee toward the company's success. And better to reward the whole staff when the product is delivered and the customer satisfied than just to reward the sales force when the sale is made. In most companies, after all, turning in the sales order is only the start of the job.

At our company, we consider success dependent upon both output and profit. Hourly workers are directly responsible for output, and management is responsible for seeing we make a profit. So we set up a two-pronged incentive program: for the workforce, a sales commission based on output; for management, profit sharing.

The hourly workforce gets a commission based on gross sales every month, whether or not we make a profit. This commission not only rewards effort but also builds in responsibility and stewardship, because output depends upon good maintenance practices, inventory levels, and management of all the details that affect output.

Because we are a custom-design shop, we quote almost every job, so we are constantly balancing profit and capacity. Management could reduce profit margins enough to have all the work in the world. But we want every order to have a good profit center and we still want enough work to keep the production force busy. A profit-sharing incentive encourages management both to see that work gets to the shop and to still maintain a profit.

In essence, we reward everybody, including the housekeeping staff, because we know the success of the company depends upon not just the sales department but everyone.

Avoid Internal Competition

Another common mistake in creating incentives is to set up internally competitive programs that reward individuals but, in the process, hurt the company by undermining cooperation among employees. Contests rewarding the highest sales often damage working relationships and the company. "I don't have time to handle this call from my customer. Can you do it for me?" one salesperson might say to another.

Is the second salesperson going to be eager to do work that contributes to his fellow employee's success? Instead, he might sabotage that competitor by even shooing away the customer.

It sounds trivial. Nevertheless, I have reviewed situations in which an owner complained his employees were adversarial. When I looked at the incentive system, I saw it was designed in such a way that divisiveness in the workforce was an obvious byproduct. It is much better to create incentives that benefit the whole group. After all, everyone contributes to the bottom line.

Keep Managing

Another mistake managers sometimes make is to assume, once an incentive program is in place, they won't have to manage that part of the business as closely. But no incentive program will ever replace the need for good management. Remember, too, values within a company change, products change and, of course, employees change, so incentive programs must be adapted to fit different circumstances.

Base Incentives on Controllable Forces

Another mistake companies commit is to make incentives too heavily dependent upon forces in the marketplace beyond the control of the employees. Remember when the Saturn division of General Motors was touted for launching a new kind of factory? Saturn compensated its employees with incentives based on sales, rather than pay a flat salary. The majority of the workforce even voted to renew the program rather than adopt a higher base pay and, for a few years, employees were several thousand dollars in incentives ahead of the salary.

But then, the Saturn automobile lost steam and sales dropped. For one thing, with gas prices down, people, not as concerned about mileage, were buying bigger cars again. So forces beyond the control of the workers affected sales, and even outstanding performance by the employees couldn't increase the incentive payment. The fact is, this particular incentive program was unduly dependent upon outside forces, on Fate.

Fate Strikes

Now, I'm going to tell you how an environmental change affected our incentive system, a change that had nothing to do with me or how good the incentive system was. In the 1980s, when high inflation gripped the economy, our incentive program looked great. Employees loved it, because inflation drove commissions up, regardless of whether we were producing and selling more.

We rode that inflationary horse up, up, up into the double digits — 15 percent, 18 percent, 20+ percent! And I looked like an extremely generous employer.

But when inflation started to back down, I started to look like Scrooge. The country went into a recession, I would say even a depression, because we were getting less than we'd gotten previously for similar products. And as inflation receded to 3 percent, the salary increase became a smaller portion of the overall income package, even though we didn't change a thing about the program. That caused trouble.

During inflation, we couldn't give raises that just matched inflation to people who were growing in ability and worth or who were taking on additional responsibilities. But people who received raises of 7 to 10 percent attributed all of it to merit, rather than account for inflation.

So in the new environment of deflation, the inflationary factor of the raise dropped in proportion to the merit factor. The merit portion didn't change, but it looked insignificant. Employees thought that they were not performing as well, that they were not being rewarded as handsomely as before. Their egos deflated and, understandably, we had a problem with low morale and discontentment.

This is a good example of why you should not do things to people without explanation. Employees were having problems figuring out the new economic reality. I studied the issue, and I trained my managers in what to say: "Look, inflation now is only 3 percent. Out of your raise of 7 percent, 4 percent – more than half – is based on merit. When we gave you a raise of 11 percent earlier, the 4 percent based on merit was only a little more than a third of it. Inflation, something we couldn't do anything about, accounted for more than half."

So many things affect incentive programs. Fate, indeed, is fickle, and you need patience – and compassion – to help your workers understand the bigger picture, which at times can be very scary for them. At least economic cycles are somewhat "evenhanded." That is, they affect almost everyone, including your competitors.

Performance Reviews

Employee performance reviews are important for several reasons, among them these three: Employees want to know how they are doing. They want to know you are considering their welfare. And they want to know you are paying them in accordance with their value to the rest of the group. They may not put it in quite those terms, but that's what they mean by "fair."

Don't set arbitrary goals. Consider what you think an employee reasonably can achieve, then measure the outcome. In fact, involve the employee in designing his growth plan, if you can. Give him a good opportunity to experience success.

Regular Evaluations

The frequency with which we evaluate employees reflects the transition from new worker to experienced worker. We conduct regular evaluations of performance based on the employee's length of tenure or length of time in a new position. The first year an employee is with us, we evaluate performance semi-annually. From then on, we evaluate once a year.

We ask all the department heads to comment on everyone in our organization for evaluations, because most of our employees interact across department lines. We give every department head a list of the people to be evaluated, and we allow each department head to make comments about that person. We never ask employees to comment on their peers. Upper management looks at the information and, if we see something that bears further scrutiny, we investigate discreetly.

Performance evaluations are more than a scrutiny of the employee. They also are an opportunity for employees to discuss complaints. Often, problems people think they have with their supervisor are mere misunderstandings that disappear if the employees just talk out their concerns with the supervisor. In fact, most of the time, having the immediate supervisor do the evaluations gets rid of those day-to-day issues that might be just little irritations. However, if an employee has a serious grievance with his supervisor, he can go to his supervisor's supervisor.

In reality, we are evaluating the supervisor and ourselves every time we evaluate the employee.

"How Am I Doing?"

When an employee asks me how I think he's doing, my first response usually is, "How do *you* think you're doing?" Most often, people don't come to a supervisor with that question, unless something is bothering them. Perhaps co-workers have made comments or some other disconcerting event has occurred. Perhaps he isn't getting enough feedback from anyone. But the employee isn't looking to you for criticism; he's looking for guidance and reassurance.

It's easy to say something judgmental. But if I were to answer his question only as it was asked, whether I give him a positive or a negative response, I miss an opportunity to learn about him and to teach him, because I have cut short communication. A positive response – "I think you're doing just fine" – doesn't tell me anything about him. A negative response doesn't either, and it may undermine our relationship, if I intimidate or shame him.

As a leader, use situations like this to get the person to talk, so you can find out what he really wants and needs. This requires serious listening, what I call "hard-rock mining." It takes a lot of effort and patience, but the more you know, the better manager you can be for him. You might gain some insight into what motivates him. You might learn about how he views his situation and the company. You might learn more about his weaknesses and where he needs additional subsidy. You might learn about his strengths and how you can enlarge his responsibilities.

If you can understand him, you are more able to provide stepping-stones for him to get through the problem he's having. You might even be able to strengthen your relationship with someone who will become the biggest supporter of your next project.

Promotions

Some people can handle situations several degrees off course, and some people can't. Generally, people who can deal with things that are out of the norm are more promotable. Those for whom everything has to be strictly by the book, those who can't deal with anything extraordinary, are not as promotable, and they will limit themselves in their work life.

Move Up the Ranks

We prefer to promote an employee rather than hire someone outside the company, and we will do a lot to try to promote from within our group. If an employee expresses interest and has the potential yet lacks some skills, we provide additional training.

But we don't force an employee into a promotion. In fact, some of our employees have declined a promotion, because they didn't think it was worth the additional stress. Others just didn't want the challenge or didn't feel comfortable being put in charge of their friends in the work group.

One of the biggest issues with promotions is recognizing that employees feel strongly about them. If more than one employee is being considered for a position (usually only one or two are seriously competing), we talk with the competitors to explain why we are offering the position to someone else.

There are times when an employee believes he's qualified but doesn't know enough about the job to understand what it requires. If we hire someone else, especially an outsider, without explaining to the employee why that employee wasn't considered, we risk losing that member of our community. At the least, we might lose his cooperation and support. So preventing – or smoothing – ruffled feathers is an important part of the process.

Promotion Reviews

By the time a person is considered for promotion, he probably will be used to a yearly evaluation. But if the promotion carries an extensive shift in responsibility, we likely would return to a semi-annual review schedule. Most importantly, we want the employee to be comfortable with when and how the evaluation takes place. We want to put him at ease, so when it occurs, he doesn't get the signal, wrongly, that he's had a setback in performance.

Preventive Maintenance

If something goes wrong with an employee, the most important step is to document what happens, so you can determine if an event is an isolated occurrence or part of a trend. The incident may not happen again, but the evidence in the file reminds you that the employee had a problem and that you should watch for a recurrence.

When employees have problems, other employees may assume the role of counselor. Some of the worst advice can come from this source, and supervisors should intervene immediately to cut it off. We have contracted with an employee-assistance firm, from which professional, private counseling is always available.

The Right Kind of Counsel

At our company, an errant employee's supervisor documents what's happening, discusses the matter with the employee, and puts notes into the employee's folder to review, if necessary, at the next evaluation. If speaking to the employee doesn't work and other efforts fail, the supervisor will take the issue to his own superior, who then will call in the errant individual to discuss the situation.

Perhaps an employee, concerned that his marriage is dissolving, is taking out his frustration and anger on co-workers. The higher-level supervisor might recommend counseling or some other intervention. His advice might even be an ultimatum. If someone's personal life is threatening to disintegrate, the last thing he should want to lose is the security of a job.

Sometimes people will quit rather than seek help. In effect, they "fire" themselves; we don't have to do it. When an employee recovers his equilibrium and resumes his job with full attention, we are gratified to know we've done a good deed. Helping an employee pull himself out of his emotional wreckage is a satisfying use of managerial authority. The practical justification: Retaining an employee is much cheaper than hiring a new one.

Helping Employees Leave

An employee who wants to leave is an employee on a mission. You can try to put all kinds of incentives in his path – growth, new jobs, different challenges – but, barring serious problems or disgruntlements with the job, what he needs is simply different scenery.

We used to go to a lot of trouble rearranging circumstances for employees whose time had come for them to leave. We made special provisions for them, tried different things, but usually, the fix was only temporary. Once they had it in their mind to leave, they soon did.

An employee whose internal alarm clock has rung often will use insignificant issues, rather than reason, to try to justify a job change. One of the signs that an employee needs a change of companies is that, in his eyes, you are bad. So when an employee becomes critical of you and his fellow workers, look at his employment history for frequency of job change. If his internal alarm clock has gone off, don't try to entice him to stay. Just help him exit gracefully.

Exit Interviews

If someone quits, we conduct an exit interview. We want to learn why the person is leaving. Some people aren't willing to talk immediately, so we ask, "If I call you in 90 days, would you talk to me about it?" Generally, they'll say yes.

If we terminate someone, we don't much care what his opinion is. Usually, we've had enough of his opinion.

When an Employee Outgrows the Company

If we only occasionally need some of the skills a person has, we have to decide whether we want to pay for those skills all the time. If we do not, then we may have to tell the employee, "You have gone beyond the skills we need. If you want to continue to increase your salary based on your skills, you should look for work someplace else, because we do not need the additional skills you have." That rarely happens, though.

Termination

When I was a kid, my grandma and grandpa had an apple orchard on their farm. To have fruit to eat throughout the winter, we used to pick apples at the farm and store them in a big, old barrel in our basement.

"Putting them by," as Mom called it, was a simple process. We'd tear out pages from an old *Sears & Roebuck* or *Montgomery Ward* catalog (not a new one, because a catalog was a precious link from our rural life to the marketplace) and wrap each apple individually before we put it into the barrel. The reason for wrapping the apples was, if one rotted, it wouldn't spoil the others as quickly if it wasn't touching them. The catalog paper separated the apples and isolated the bad ones.

I remember that story when I consider the unfortunate need to terminate employees. Termination helps protect the welfare of the group and the company. Ultimately, we let people go because they "spoil" the workplace. That is, they cause problems for their co-workers, disrupt the job setting with unprofessional behavior or, in other ways, don't or won't measure up to reasonable standards.

The other employees look to management to do something about the problem individual. They may not ask us to do it, but they expect us to do it, to protect them. They think that's part of our job. And it is.

Termination is a last resort. Admittedly, instances occur in which an employee takes a turn for the worse because of something outside management's jurisdiction, a personal problem, for example, that intrudes on the workplace and that the employee doesn't remedy.

But termination also can be an admission of management's failure, when it occurs because someone was hired inappropriately in the first place or because management made mistakes along the way in overseeing the employee. Whatever the reason, when termination of an employee occurs, it should be carried out with compassion, without emotionalism, and within a standard process.

The Standard Process

Don't do what one foreman I once knew, when I worked for another company, used to do. He was a passive guy. When he got upset with somebody, he'd nurse a grudge against that person and build a case for termination. He gave no warning to the employee. In fact, he'd tell me only about five minutes before he was going to let someone go. I'd have to scurry to get a last check ready.

He always terminated employees on a Friday and gave them their check on the way out the door. It was a terrible way to treat them. I knew I'd never allow that when I owned my own company.

Let me repeat: Termination is a last resort. At our company, it occurs usually after we have warned the employee several times, documented instances of the problem, and tried to intervene in whatever ways seemed appropriate. Only if an employee commits an egregious offense, such as blatant sexual harassment, which is clearly forbidden and noted in our employee handbook, would we terminate the person immediately.

An employee who doesn't square himself away leaves management no choice but to let him go. However, no supervisor individually terminates an employee. To give the person every possible consideration, a committee of three people in management reviews the circumstances and confirms the need for the termination. Above all, we want to be sure no supervisor acts in a fit of reactionary rage. Termination should be not an emotional reaction but the result of a rational and objective process.

Often, even after all the trouble, all the warnings, all the urgent recommendations to use the employee-assistance program, a terminated employee seems surprised. He wants to know why. At this point, the worst thing you can do is try to justify the termination. He won't agree with you, and trying to get him to see your reasoning will only aggravate the situation.

We take a lot of time to decide about terminating an employee, so once we've gone through the whole process and the committee of three people has agreed to the termination, we proceed. Thus, having exercised due diligence, we figure if we've erred, we've erred, but we're not going to debate the termination with the individual. The issue is no longer why; it's now about the employee's rights as a terminated worker.

Then we explain the process of separating him from the company, and begin settling up his wages, explaining unemployment and insurance benefits to which he is entitled, cashing in his share of incentive and pension programs, signing papers, and so forth.

Trauma

Obviously, termination is traumatic for the employee who has just lost his security, his income, his livelihood. In one company for which I worked, a terminated employee struck and knocked out the foreman who let him go. The foreman could have been killed if he'd fallen on a sharp-edged machine.

Termination also is – or should be – uncomfortable for the manager who handles the termination. Being let go hurts, and no humane person takes pleasure in inflicting pain on someone. However, the manager should take consolation in knowing he's done his job of protecting the group by separating from it a person who isn't concerned enough about the welfare of the individuals with whom he works or the welfare of the company that's employed him.

To some extent, an employee's termination also can be uncomfortable for co-workers, who now must adjust to a change in the workplace, however welcome that change. They might even be thinking, "There, but for the grace of God, go I." And so, for some days after you let someone go, many employees might treat you differently, even though the termination was a committee process and warranted. They will avoid you, out of fear they might be next.

Hang in there. As they relax and resume their normal courteous ways, they may even say to you, as I sometimes hear: "You did the right thing. He didn't deserve to work here."

How to Avoid Being Sued – or at Least Losing the Case

Employees who have been wrongly terminated have recourse in the justice system. Even employees who have been terminated appropriately can try to retaliate by suing their employer. So you probably won't escape at least the occasional attempt by an employee to retaliate. But the best defense happens before you've even hired the employee.

First, be sure you have a personnel policy handbook that your labor attorney has reviewed. It should be current and comprehensive, and it should spell out clearly the standards and the expectations you have of employees, so there is no question about what you mean or want or about what will justify letting an employee go.

Second, develop a standard process for terminating employees, and follow it for everybody.

Third, don't give an employee who's just been let go a chance to confuse the situation in a jumble of words. Managers get into trouble when they terminate employees by seeking their approval or by trying to justify the termination, and the justification fuels the court case. You don't need to explain. The events of intervention leading to the termination are fair warning.

Chapter 8
Deciphering People

At about the age of five, I graduated to scheduled livestock chores such as gathering eggs. For a little kid, that was a scary job. Normally, I just reached in and grabbed the chickens off their nests. But when a hen gets into a settin' mood, she quits laying and gets mean and protective of her eggs.

I still have the scars on my fingers from being pecked, before I learned to distract the hens with a corncob. While a hen was pecking at it, I'd grab her by the neck and pull her off the nest to get the eggs.

I also helped take care of the cattle. In June and July, we'd get permission from our neighbors to herd our cows on the sides of the road. The grass there was good enough for the cows, and using the ditches gave our pastures a chance to rejuvenate. I'd sit by the road all day, keeping the cows out of trouble.

If a car would come by, which was rare, I'd split the herd so the car could get through. I had to make sure the cows *didn't spook and run off and get hurt. I'd herd them around all day and bring them home at night.*

If a cow got down, nursing her back to health was a lot of extra work. So while I fed the cattle, I kept an eye out for any problem. Dad expected me to let him know if any of them needed special attention: "That old brown one over there doesn't look so good. You'd better take a look at her."

When I think now about the responsibility that chore entailed, I realize how much Dad trusted me.

Branding and dehorning were exciting times, especially for a little kid. As we'd herd the calves into a corral, then into a chute, I'd try to make myself as big as I could with my coat, while the calves did their best to escape by us. The main objective for us was not to get hurt in the process.

Personality Counts

Some people find the procedural chores of farm life pleasurable, even comforting. I hated them. Feeding the chickens, slopping the hogs, milking the cows day in and day out oppressed rather than soothed me. Driving the tractor up and down row after row after row of crops bored me to numbness. As a kid, I knew I would not grow up to be a farmer.

Years later, when I studied theories of personality and methods of identifying the characteristics of people, I realized I was not an intractable youngster after all – I just hated procedure. That is, I hated repetition. It turns out I prefer options, new and different tasks, problems, and challenges.

Thank goodness, options are a big part of the career I chose. I didn't know, when I decided to buy the company, I was choosing something that fit my need for options. I just knew I liked machines and making things and enjoyed designing answers to manufacturing problems.

Why to Bother

I was fortunate in my choice. Many people go into professions for which their personality or aptitudes are a poor match. Perhaps they acquiesced to a parental wish that they choose a particular career. Perhaps they had an unrealistic notion of the career they selected. Perhaps they chose their profession for some other wrong motivation.

The reason doesn't matter. What does matter is that the results can be disappointment, frustration, and squandered potential. The poor souls may struggle for years to find fulfillment in their life's work, never realizing it's the wrong work for them.

Learning to identify personality characteristics has helped me more clearly understand myself and my motivations. More to the point, it has helped me more clearly understand others.

I am a better manager, because I now have ways to interpret the language and behavior of my employees, ways that give me a more realistic and more accurate picture of them. I can communicate better with them, because I understand better what communication process they, perhaps unknowingly, prefer. With what I know about their individual personality traits, I am better able to help them succeed.

I believe most employees, at least on the first day, want to please their supervisor and to do well. If the rosy outlook fades to gray, we, as managers, may bear some of the blame, because we don't understand them well enough to lead them effectively.

Get a Grip on Reality

It's easy to judge others when they are different from what we consider appropriate. But when you are trying to understand someone, making value judgments is unfair and beside the point. Identifying personality characteristics is not about good versus bad. It's about such concerns as whether an individual's personality traits are appropriate for the job, how best to motivate an employee, how best to get your point across.

No doubt, personality profiling is subjective, because it involves judgment calls, interpretations, and opinions about abstract qualities. That's why psychological tests are rated for their *validity*, which expresses how precisely they identify the characteristics they are meant to identify, and their *reliability*, which expresses how consistently the answers reflect the correct interpretation.

But we're better off trying to explain personality traits with an objective system of agreed-upon nomenclature than simply reacting emotionally to some factor we can't even name. A system gives us a frame of reference.

Remember, though, different screening devices use different "templates" to describe personality traits. In addition, different resources may use the same term, "introvert," for example, but apply different definitions. When you are considering personality qualities, be clear about which definition you mean and to which trait-differentiation devices you are referring.

Remember, too, that it's better to discuss motivations, traits, and personality preferences in terms of tentative observations, tendencies, and possibilities. Our perception of someone is our interpretation of what we observe and experience. New information might alter our perception.

With the ability to categorize personality traits, a new world opens. We see characteristics that, before, were beyond our awareness. We notice patterns. We can interpret actions more appropriately. Just as it is ridiculous to expect a cat to behave like a bird, so is it futile to expect people to change the basic characteristics of their personality.

Accepting that reality, we stop wasting precious time and energy and start focusing on how we can make the information useful.

The Personality of a Job

Just as individuals have certain personality traits, careers and jobs also tend to have a set of personality requirements. Take the career of an elementary school teacher and that of a college professor, for example. You wouldn't expect them to have a similar psychological profile.

Consider the situations. The grade school teacher has to interact with active little children, who need and demand constant attention. The teacher has to coddle them, care for them, wipe away their tears, and give them lots of encouragement. The world of these little charges is black and white, so simple and quick decisions are best.

College professors, on the other hand, teach, yes, but classes may be hundreds of students in an auditorium – an impersonal setting – and such professors do not necessarily interact much with students. Professors may teach not for the fulfillment of teaching itself, necessarily, but to learn. And their learning is never complete.

A person with the psychological profile of a kindergarten teacher probably would feel isolated in a college auditorium-classroom. Someone with the psychological typing of a college professor would feel uncomfortable in a kindergarten.

So one of the most important steps in creating a good workforce is figuring out the attributes necessary for the positions you need to fill. I suggest you consider the following characteristics.

Proactive/Reactive

Does the job require a person to be proactive or reactive? This consideration is one of the most important. It refers to whether the person is called upon to make things happen, or to respond or wait for instructions. In extreme terms, an arsonist is proactive; a firefighter is reactive.

We tend to be proactive about some things and reactive about other things in our lives. But you especially want to know whether the person is primarily proactive or reactive in a job setting, to match what the job itself requires.

For instance, you might think the position of receptionist is a reactive job. But consider what you expect from your receptionist. Do you require the person perhaps to assess the needs of people coming through the door and to direct those visitors to the appropriate place? Does the receptionist need to schedule appointments, take care of payments from clients and send out notices? Or do you expect the person simply to be polite and answer the phone?

If the job requires proactivity, but you hire a person who isn't proactive in that situation, things you want done won't get done. If, on the other hand, you need someone who will wait for instructions or who can wait for something to happen before acting, hiring a proactive individual might make you feel as if you've lost control.

Inclusionary/Exclusionary

Consider whether the job requires someone who is inclusionary or exclusionary – or some of both. Inclusionary people are open to other people and to ideas and like to involve others in their projects. Jobs requiring active interaction with people, such as sales and public relations positions, require inclusionary types.

Exclusionary people tend to be cautious, critical, and discriminating. They tend to avoid, looking for problems and reasons to exclude. They run everything through the filter of what's wrong. They would look at a batch of parts and say, "I don't want that piece," instead of saying, "Boy, that batch looks good. Go with it."

Jobs that require discrimination and attention to quality require exclusionary types. For instance, investigative accounting jobs require an exclusionary person, someone who doesn't accept things at face value, because he's trying to find out why events occurred.

The Source of Approval

Does the job include feedback or is it a "thankless" one? Some people want to be told by others how they're doing. Some "just know" they're doing a good job (whether or not they actually are).

That's an important interview issue, because a person who knows within himself he's doing a good job can function in a "thankless" position, where responses to his efforts are few. But a person who relies on outside input about how he's doing will feel frustrated in a setting where he gets little of it. He doesn't necessarily need feedback in person. A written report or a tip for good service might scratch the itch.

Options/Procedures

Does the job you want to fill require a person who invents new ways to do things, or do you need someone who prefers to follow procedures? For the purpose of this discussion, we'll describe people who look for new ways as options oriented. People who say, "This is the way it's done, and we're going to keep doing it this way," we'll call procedural.

People who prefer options look for choices. They like to come up with new processes, even in unimportant situations. For instance, they might take a different route to work each day.

Procedural people wake the world. They distribute the newspapers. They walk the dog. They put on the coffee. They open the shop. They are comfortable with routine and with familiar processes. Procedural people will even try to impose a procedure that works in one situation onto another situation, because they default to the routine.

My employees have helped me realize the importance of the distinction between options and procedures. Many welders who applied to work for us said they were bored with their previous job. When we hired them, I expected them eventually to get bored working for us, too, but they didn't. On the contrary, they seemed contented.

As I began to study personality types, I soon understood why these employees thrived at my company. They, like me, were motivated by options. The procedural work in their old jobs, welding the same things the same ways, burned them out. In our shop, where each project is different, they liked having to make choices about how to do their job. Even a seemingly procedural job, such as welding, can have optional aspects.

Difference/Sameness

Consider how fast the position you want to fill evolves. Does it lean toward changing or toward staying the same? A job oriented toward change requires a person who likes the new, who looks for the unique – a "difference" person. He doesn't mind sudden, revolutionary change. On the other hand, a job where things change little requires a person who prefers the status quo. This kind of person likes the same neighborhood, the same job, the same activities for long periods. This person is more comfortable with evolutionary adjustment, if there is to be any change.

Then there are those between these two extremes.

Look beyond the job description to the activities in the job. For instance, you might think an accountant would be inclined toward sameness. But an accountant who develops new accounting procedures is going to prefer some change. A person with such expertise is not going to be like the person who does the actual accounting, a sameness person.

I like to put it this way: The person who builds the railroad rarely is the one who can run it. Building a railroad involves making many decisions about a situation that is constantly evolving on a huge scale.

To maintain consistency, the business of running a railroad, once built, falls into a pattern that requires commitment to policies, procedures, and schedules. These two situations highlight the distinction between difference and sameness in a job.

General/Specific

Does the job require a general approach or great attention to detail? Generalists, interested in the overview of things, look for what stands out. "Specifics" like exactness and need details.

When you are considering which characteristics a job requires, think about how much specificity the job entails. An engraver's job is more specific than that of a housepainter, whose job is more detailed than a truck driver's. A supervisory position is probably general, a computer-programming position most likely specific.

Some jobs can lean toward either preference. You might think an estimator's job is specific but, in fact, some jobs require a general estimator. Let's say you have 10 machines and they are going to form a system requiring interaction among them. The person you want to estimate that project would be more of a generalist than the person estimating a highly detailed precision job in a machine shop.

Loner/Joiner

Does the job require working alone or with others? Consider whether the applicant likes to work independently or in a group. Don't put somebody who needs group dynamics into a job where he's working independently and isolated.

For a job requiring interaction with others, don't hire an independent type who, when four people need to talk to him, is likely to say, "Leave me alone, I have work to do," and close his door. If you're looking for a supervisor, you want a person who enjoys working with people and, especially, who feels responsible for the outcome of the group's efforts.

Expressive/Low-Key

Does the job or position require someone who's expressive or someone who's placid? That is, does the person need to be animated or low-key? This issue may not be important for the job itself, but if the department consists of people who sharpen their pencils, work steadily, and keep their noses down, adding someone who talks all the time may cause problems. A person's interactive style can violate others. If you have two people equally qualified, fit the personality to that of the group.

Who's To Blame?

Watch the individual who blames others for all his problems. If he does, then you, as his employer, are likely to become one of the "reasons" for what goes wrong in his life.

People/Things

Does the job require working mainly with people or with things? Ask an applicant a question like: What did you like about your last job? Someone who speaks about other people and working with them is a "people person." Someone who talks mostly about ideas, systems, tools, or places is oriented to things.

Feeling/Thinking

Does the job require empathy, or does it require just considering facts? For Heaven's sake, don't put a person who's interested only in facts into a job that requires attention to the feelings of others. For instance, a "fact" person in the complaint department of a retail business is likely to think: Look, we didn't drive you here and make you buy this; you keep it.

A person who is empathetic, on the other hand, can listen to customers and relate to them rather than make them mad. An empathetic person says, "I understand how you feel, but the company's position is . . . Let me try to fix things so I make you happy and keep the company happy."

The Real Story

The words a person uses to tell his story in an interview say more about his personality preferences, traits, and motivations than does the story itself. I was once on an interview committee to hire a principal for a grade school. One of the applicants used "I" throughout the interview, until we came to the topic of moving to Omaha. Then he began saying "we," in reference to someone who, he said, would help make the decision.

When the other interviewers left the room to tend to some chores, I leaned over to him and asked, "Who's 'we'?" "We" was his dog and he.

Now, the words our interviewee used made a strong impression on me. They reinforced my belief in the importance of listening to the words themselves. "I" and "we" told completely different stories, once I learned whom they represented. The man initially came across as extremely independent, but including his dog in the decision to move caused me to question whether he would assume responsibility for major decisions on the job.

More Than the Résumé

In addition to listening carefully, you of course will scrutinize the applicant's job history. Look not only for facts but also for patterns of profession and tenure.

Ask about job settings and the aspects about them the person enjoyed. Are they similar to conditions of the position the applicant is seeking? Did the applicant follow procedures in previous jobs, or did he have to come up with new solutions frequently? Did he work alone? Did he work around others or in a team?

Ask about the kinds of decisions the person had to make. For instance, did he respond to circumstances or make things happen?

Ask how he knows he's doing a good job.

Be Careful

We can't directly see atoms or molecules; we can only know about them by observing the results of their actions. Neither can we really know a person completely and with certainty. At best, we can only make assumptions, based on what we observe and perceive.

Still, we have to start somewhere, and many of the personality differentiating systems available today are helpful in figuring out what our fellow human beings, as well as we, are about. But observations are always tentative, always pending additional information. If we can remember that, we can avoid boxing people into absolute descriptions that limit our understanding of them and our options for the ways we interact with them.

Chapter 9
Managing Your Capital Assets

For several days, Dad had been leaving in the early morning with our two mares, Flossie and Fanny, and a hayrack and returning late at night. He was part of a threshing bee, a group of farmers helping each other thresh their grain, which had been dried and shocked in the fields.

Buster Durst owned a steam-powered thresher, which he took to each farm in turn. The cooperating farmers brought their hayracks and wagons to carry the shocks of grain to the machine and the seed grain away from it.

One evening, Dad returned home and announced to Mom, "We're done with the Durst place. They're coming to our place next." I heard, but I didn't fully understand what that would mean. What I did know was that Buster was on his way to our farm with the threshing machine so it would be ready first thing in the morning.

I vividly remember that evening. It was hot and the southeast wind was no relief, especially with all the excitement. Nothing matches a little kid's anticipation: Wow! The threshing machine is going to be here all night, and in just a little while, I'll be able to crawl all over it. And maybe Buster will bring Donnie (his son, who was about my age and fun to play with).

I ran as far as I dared up the road, barely within earshot of Mom, to watch for this great thing I had been hearing and wondering about. Finally, a huffing and puffing, a wheezing that seemed to come from miles away, forecast the arrival of the thresher. Then a whole train of equipment busted through the sunset.

That machinery was so immense, so powerful, so unstoppable, so noisy, so complicated, so beautiful, so wonderful! I was awestruck as Buster drove up the road toward our house. He turned into our lane, our very lane. Barefoot, I ran alongside as fast as I could in the sand and sandburs.

Buster brought the thresher into our yard, then shut down the steam engine. It made awesome sounds as it put itself to rest, after the fire was put out and as the steam cooled to water. I was warned: "Don't touch it; it's hot. Don't climb up on it. Don't touch any of the levers." I didn't mind. Even the admonishments impressed upon me the power and the beauty of that colossal machine.

The next day, I watched as Buster lit the fire in the steam engine and as the water again turned to steam and the steam again started to produce power. The click-clack and the huff-puff and the bang-bang and the sparks all created unique and wondrous sensations for me.

The crew set up the threshing machine by the barn, so the straw could be blown into the haymow, the chaff could be separated from the grain, and the grain could flow into the grain bin.

I watched as all the farmers who were part of the threshing crew arrived at our house with their horses and their wagons and their hayracks. Soon they all were out in the fields gathering the bundles of grain in their hayracks, competing with *each other to see who could pile bundles the highest and whose horses could pull the most.*

I also watched Buster, and I realized something important: The guy who owned the threshing machine wasn't doing the hard, sweaty, dirty physical labor. No. He was giving orders. Every once in a while he'd walk over to tighten the tensioning device on a belt on the threshing machine or adjust the steam vents. And all along he'd exercise his authority about how the threshing machine was run. But he hardly got dirty.

That image had an effect on me, as I lugged water bottles, weighing more than I did, with my little red wagon for half a mile through the sand to the hot and sweaty men. That singular event said to me: Look at the power of owning equipment.

I saw that all those farmers needed Buster and his machine. They respected him. A few no doubt feared him, for he even decided who would be on the threshing crew. A man who was considered lazy or whose wife was not a good cook (the women prepared big lunches for the workers) might not be invited to join the threshing crew the next year. That farmer then was left to find other means of threshing his grain.

I saw that the man who owned the machinery controlled what was going to happen, he got paid to do it, and he had the respect of the community.

Formula for Success

Buster Durst's success came from owning equipment others needed. He used a simple formula: Capability plus opportunity equals success.

Note that capability comes first. If you concentrate on capability, you will be more proactive in trying to find ways to put that capability to work for you. And when you put it to work, the company grows almost automatically. Select a machine or other capital investment you think has potential in the marketplace, then go out and look for the opportunity to capture that potential.

Expanding Capability

All the growth I have achieved has been about expanding our capability, so when opportunities came along, we could take advantage of them. For example, during one downturn, we put all our effort into computerizing our job-costing process.

Another time, we invested in technology and developed software programs to do layouts of fundamental shapes, such as cones and elbows. We had always worked with these difficult shapes in engineering design projects, and I didn't see any reason why we wouldn't work with them in the future.

When the market recovered and opportunity returned, we were able to make components, such as cones and elbows, faster than our competitors and with better accuracy and less preparation time.

Let me give you another example of the importance of investing in capability. When I bought the company, it was a tiny one. I paid about $85,000 for all the equipment and inventory, though I probably could have gotten only about $50,000 for everything at auction. The equipment didn't have capabilities I thought we needed, so I designed the "perfect" machine for my business and hired a tool-and-die maker to help me build it.

While we were discussing how to build this machine, I came across a little announcement about a numerically controlled (NC) single-station punch press. It had a plasma-arc option (it could thermally burn out patterns), which made the machine much more versatile than an ordinary NC punch press. It could cut out patterns in profile. We had been cutting patterns by drawing a line on a piece of metal and sawing or burning the profile by hand, a dangerous and inconsistent process. It was my perfect machine.

What I'm trying to say is, I determined our business needs and developed a vision of how we could meet those needs with a machine I was prepared to build. When the real thing came along, I didn't need any convincing, because I already had the solution in mind – a plan, if you will. It was something I already knew would be the best thing for my business.

With that machine, we could make repetitive parts with precision at a fraction of the cost of the way we traditionally made them and, more importantly, cheaper and faster than our competition made them.

Financing Capability

Wanting to invest in capability is one thing; financing that investment is another. By 1976, when I had owned my company for only about four years, I had established a good track record with my bank. I had proven I could manage the business at least as well as the previous owner had, I could grow it faster, and I could manage my loans. So I went to my banker and asked to borrow the $150,000 I needed to buy the NC punch press.

After he coughed his tongue back up, I laid out all the paperwork, showed him pictures of the machine, told him what the machine would do, and explained how it would affect profitability. I convinced him we were moving from an era of hand-eye-tool coordination into an electronic age. I described how a new kind of employee was evolving and a different group was emerging. I convinced him the effects of this investment were timely and futuristic.

My presentation proved to him, rather than trying to solve a problem with that machine, I was creating capability. He could see that potential and he approved the loan.

That decision probably wasn't too tough for him to make. First of all, most machine tools have a good aftermarket value.

Second, because the market was suffering through inflationary times, waiting even a couple of months would only have meant we'd pay more for the machine. Still, we were spending on this one machine close to three times the value of the rest of the equipment we had in the company.

How much a machine costs compared with what you already have doesn't matter much. What matters more is how useful and how productive it can become. In other words, the issue is not so much what the item may cost; the issue is how much it improves your capability. When I bought the NC punch press, it cost more than the value of the company's entire inventory of machinery, but it significantly enhanced our rate of growth.

Expanding the Company

In a short time we tripled our size, because the NC punch press and other related capital improvements so greatly enhanced our capability. We continue to buy for the future.

The new building we put up in 1999 doubled the capacity of our factory and increased our office capacity as well. We don't have the staff or the business to fill it right away. In fact, that expansion will be a parasite to some of our profits for the next few years. But our experience has been that, by increasing our capacity, we are ready for opportunities that come our way.

The Case for Buying Equipment

If you don't buy new goods and equipment and rotate out the old, you will end up with no deductible depreciation – a double whammy, because at the same time that you aren't replenishing your old equipment, you continue to pay higher taxes, and you suffer from lower potential productivity than what a new machine could provide.

Continually rotating or upgrading your equipment is a good idea, but there are some considerations to keep in mind. Of course, you have to look at the net value you will get from such an investment to determine whether it's worthwhile at a given time. On occasion, we have rented equipment rather than buy it, because we needed it only temporarily or infrequently. We knew investing in that equipment would not be productive.

When we were in an era of high inflation and tax credits for investments in capital equipment, buying equipment was almost a no-brainer. Waiting only meant the machinery would be much more expensive, and we would have been foolish to pass up the tax advantages. In times of low inflation, making such investment decisions is more difficult and less forgiving, because the dollars with which we pay off our loans are harder to earn.

Another factor to consider when you are thinking about buying equipment is whether that equipment, particularly high-tech items, will be cheaper in the near future. As new and improved versions, with cheaper components and more computing power, rush onto the market, a lot of equipment becomes obsolete sooner, and knowing when the rate of improvements has slowed appreciably enough to justify the investment at a particular point can be difficult. Read, ask, find a consultant.

You may be better off upgrading what you have. For instance, we have an old shear in perfect shape. It cost me about $80,000 when I bought it 25 years ago. Rather than replace it with newer and better machines through the years, I've have been able to improve that old machine and make it more productive. We've added a conveyor and a numerically controlled front gauge that makes it more automated.

We've virtually doubled the cost of the machine, but we've gotten a lot of that money back through depreciation, money we otherwise would have paid in taxes. More importantly, with this machine and its improvements, we can make parts more efficiently and of better quality.

In addition, because a person can produce much more on that shear, we have been able to control workforce inflation, which occurs when workers receive raises without a corresponding increase in production.

Consider how the purchase of new equipment will affect your cash flow. You might be able to justify a higher cost for a machine that will increase your production throughput significantly. And, of course, think about how your purchase of new equipment will affect the components of service to your customers.

Look Past the Price

Many salespeople, when they make their presentation, default to lowest price, because it's such a good purchase trigger. But if you want to stretch your money the furthest, look past the price. Consider the quality you're paying for instead of which is cheapest – or most expensive.

Think of the relative values of good, better, and best. Often, the overall value buy is not in "good," nor in "best." "Good" might have cheaper bearings and a basic paint job. "Best" might have better internal features and a prettier cowling or a shinier paint job that offers no additional functional value. "Better" might have the internal features of "Best" inside a case that's just adequate rather than pretty. Where's the best value for your dollar?

I look carefully at the "better" market, sometimes prodding the salesperson, who is used to customers who respond to competitive pricing or the snob appeal of buying the best.

Employees and Equipment

Investing in machines augments the value of the individual, by increasing the individual's output, whether through quantity or quality. I saw that happen when Buster Durst brought his steam-powered threshing machine to our fields. I saw it happen when I convinced my boss at the steel company where I worked to buy a tapping machine that enhanced consistency and reduced the number of rejected parts.

At the same time, I regard the company employees not as dispensable business components but as members of a community I work hard to keep intact. We have built our business cautiously, to avoid volatility in the size of our workforce as the economy grows and slows. We don't have to add machines to our shop to replace our workers; instead, we add machines to enhance their capability.

I have taught employees in our company that machines will become obsolete, but people won't, if they continue to learn. In fact, we enlist the advice of our employees when we consider equipment.

When we buy a new machine, it is one the employees themselves have helped us choose. They know they will be acquiring new skills and growing in experience as they learn how to run a new piece of equipment. Consequently, they are excited about the new equipment rather than fearful it might replace them.

Management has the responsibility to research and create strategy for capital investments, and it is good policy to enlist your employees in the process. But if you want them to help you improve your inventory of equipment, you must put incentives in place that encourage them, and you must protect their jobs. Our salary program encourages our employees to keep improving efficiency and productivity. Giving them credit at their performance review is additional reward.

Cash Flow

Managing cash flow is easier if you think of it on a simple timeline. For example, accounts receivable, a short-term item usually, are cyclical.

And though some of your operating expenses may be related to that cycle, you also have to pay for ongoing overhead – salaries, utilities, supplies, and rent or mortgage payments, to name a few items.

A profitable company relies on its accounts receivable to flow predictably so as not to burden short-term funding for operating expenses. Getting paid on time and paying others on time are essential.

A healthy, growing company will have enough income set aside to pay longer-term expenses, such as capital improvements, capital equipment, investments, or insurance on executive officers. These longer-term assets enhance the net worth of the company, as well as provide a means of additional cash retention.

For instance, we invest in insurance on our executives when they are young enough that it's a good buy. Those policies amount to cash value that sits there growing. They protect the investment in our executives, but they also are a source of cash.

Investing for Growth

It's a good idea to match the value of your accounts receivable with an equal value of investments. As you plow your profits back into buying additional insurance, property, and other long-term investments, perhaps less liquid but enhancing your net worth, the long-term value of your company increases. I knew, if my company were to continue to be successful, we would need to continue to expand the size of our facility, so I purchased lots five times the size I needed for the first building. After using up half of the original lots, I was able to buy adjacent lots.

All the years of caring for this unused investment paid off: We now use 100 percent of the land. The factor that drove us to buy the land before we needed it was that moving later would cost more, because of such factors as utilities, foundations for the heavy machinery, and inflation.

One Central Account

Although you may have several bank accounts designated for different purposes, consider initially putting all your cash through one master checking account and using it as a distribution center for your funds. From there, you can transfer funds to other accounts, withdraw cash using an automated teller machine, or write checks.

Of course, you are likely to have a more elaborate general financial system, but using a master account is a good way to monitor cash flow. One quick glance at the monthly financial statement gives you an overall view of how you are spending your money.

Keep in mind, in general, accounts are federally insured up to only $100,000 per account owner (depending upon the circumstances of the account). To protect our funds, we set up our federally insured accounts under different corporate entities within our company.

Pricing and Profit

Follow this logic: By definition, charity operations are nonprofit. The first reason you are in business is to make a profit. Business is not charity.

Before setting prices, know all your costs, including the value of time. Do not price products or services lower than costs. Remember to include such items as the costs of ownership or lease of your building and equipment, the cost of your capital (another reason to keep your interest payments as low as possible), and the cost of investing in your inventory.

Some items move quickly, others don't. In the meantime, some of your capital is tied up in those low-turnover items, capital you should get paid for using. You can pass the cost of that investment along to customers by charging higher prices for low-turnover items you have to stock for your customers' convenience.

Some processes cost more than others, and those costs should be reflected in your price structure. In our business, for example, fabricating machines from stainless steel costs much more than using carbon steel. So we need to charge more to make machines from stainless steel. You legitimately deserve to get a return on your investment in materials and processes, and it is acceptable to pass your costs along to your customers.

The business environment contracts and expands. That competitive environment, and such issues as obsolete technology and training new employees, will squeeze profits often enough. So when looking at pricing, consider what the market will bear, and take advantage of opportunities to set bigger profits. (But don't be greedy.)

No one is going to come to you and out of generosity offer you more money. You have to ask for it.

Real Costs, Real Productivity

Only when you know how much your product really costs can you determine your rate of productivity and your profit. One of the major costs, of course, is what you pay your employees. Labor isn't just a basic hourly wage; conversely, the productivity you pay for at face value isn't what you actually get.

For the sake of simplicity, let's say you're paying a worker $10 an hour for an eight-hour day. Out of that day, you pay him for down time: two 15-minute breaks and a 30-minute lunch period.

At that point, you aren't paying your employee $10 an hour, because you're getting only seven hours of labor from him. You're actually paying him an hourly returnable wage of $11.43.

Then, by the time you add restroom visits, perhaps a personal phone call, a five-minute chat at the water fountain about last night's game, and other "productivity leaks," you're paying about $12.31 an hour for about six and a half hours of work. That's an increase of just over 23 percent.

Add two weeks of vacation and five holidays and you're up to more than $13 per hour in usable wages. That's another 6 percent, and we haven't even mentioned insurance premiums, workers' compensation, social security, or a pension plan.

Short-Term Tradeoffs

The market that processes beef and pork is a new marketplace for us. We're taking jobs with lower profit margins than those in our old marketplaces, to see to what level we can raise our cash flow. As we build our capability and acquire more customers, we will be choosier about which jobs we take. We know increased choices from a larger customer base will bring greater profitability, as we become more knowledgeable and efficient in serving this market. We're willing to wait for that return.

Don't Let Debt Control You

Debt, properly applied, is useful in your array of financial tools. Improperly applied, it's a wrecking ball. Stay in control of your financial situation by evaluating your debt structure regularly, continually.

In other words, keep track of how much borrowed capital you're using, whether it's from bank loans, loans against insurance policies, vendors' purchase programs, or credit cards, to name a few sources.

Not only must you know how much interest you're paying annually, but also, especially, to have a clear picture of your true financial condition, you must know what rate of interest you're paying. Compare it to the current interest rate. If yours is significantly higher, consider refinancing.

Let's say you initially got a $100,000 line of credit at 15 percent interest but the current market interest rate is now 10 percent. If you have good cash flow and you're borrowing just enough to keep your credit line active, your annual interest payment might not look like much.

But at 15 percent, the interest on $100,000 is a much bigger chunk. Few businesses can make a profit when they're paying that much interest on a high percent of their borrowed money.

Don't burden yourself with so much overhead that you become a slave to it or that you risk losing your business because you can't make the payments. Consider as a rule of thumb: Can we keep up the payments if business drops 20 percent, 25 percent, 30 percent, more?

Leaks in the Wallet

The Great Depression taught people many things, one being: don't be wasteful. But in periods of great economic prosperity, this society tends to squander tremendous amounts, little realizing that being wasteful takes away part of our spending power. It's a leak in the wallet.

Indiscriminate spending, likewise, is another kind of wastefulness. Some people spend money as if they have discretionary income, when they don't – and they never will if they keep buying things they don't need and can't afford.

When I was on a strict budget and saw something I wanted, I would ask myself, Do I really need it? Every time I went to a hardware store, I would have to ask that question over and over, because stuff in hardware stores is hard for me to resist. To this day, I can't go into a hardware store without being tempted.

One exercise I used in making my decision about buying something was to consider how many hours I would have to work, after taxes, to pay for that item. Making $10 an hour and taking home, say, $7, the issue became: Is that scroll saw worth four hours of my labor, or would I be better off putting that money into my savings account? Of course, this same approach can be applied to the corporate level of spending.

Convenience has a value, but buying for convenience is a luxury, unless you can economically justify that convenience. Think about how it will affect your cash flow. Many times outsourcing, even though not convenient, is the right answer.

Loan interest is a big leak in the wallet, and credit cards are an insidious source of this kind of leak. Step back from the monthly payments to look at the overall cost of your purchase. A small monthly payment can disguise the real cost. If your average monthly balance is $2,500, and your annual percentage rate (APR) is 18, you'll pay an additional $450 a year, not counting any annual fees or late charges. Is what you bought worth that extra cost?

Are You Frugal or Miserly?

To budget appropriately for your needs and wants is one thing; to be stingy with your cash, even for yourself and your family, is quite another. Frugality is not a virtue if it degrades you. Pinching pennies unnecessarily is not in your best interest if it causes hardship to your family or company, places your future in financial jeopardy, or puts you in substandard or unsafe circumstances.

Paying yourself a substandard salary, for example, may make you feel like you're saving money at the time. But if it means that, in retirement, you'll receive lower social security benefits, which are based on your "paid in" history, you'll be sorry. You might be better off paying yourself a salary that guarantees optimum benefits.

If your place of business looks like the dickens, you do yourself a disservice by presenting a disheveled setting. In the long run, you would be better off, even if you borrowed money, to improve the looks of your business and your public image, rather than try to operate on the cheap.

Invest your money where it will do you the most good. That may be in the bank or the stock market, in equipment or company improvements – or it might be in a newer car or in clothes that improve your own appearance.

Of course, you need money to survive day to day, but remember, too, you will need money to survive in the future. Budget so as to contribute to your savings, in some form, every month.

Return on Investment

Generally, when I spend cash, for whatever purpose, I look at cost and the potential return on investment, by considering the value I'm getting for my money. Am I buying immediate usefulness, preventive measures, inherent worth, a promising future yield?

I think of my expenditures in two terms: first, what I should spend money on and, second, what I should quit spending money on. I keep a list of needs, for which I set priorities, using this matrix, discussed more fully in the "Efficiency" chapter: vital and urgent; not vital but urgent; vital but not urgent; not vital and not urgent. You want to get into a situation in which your expenditure is "vital but not urgent." Repairing a leaky roof, if inventory is being ruined, is "vital and urgent." A new conference room might be "vital but not urgent."

Certain things have intrinsic value and are worth maintaining regardless of cost. For example, I wouldn't scrimp on the appearance of my company, the buildings, the real property. But, generally, I look down the road to avoid "vital and urgent" situations because, if I need something vital and urgent, I'm not going to be able to buy it at a competitive price. Any time you find yourself in an "urgent" situation, the price goes up.

Keep Control of Your Cash

All things being equal, I don't want to spend one more dime than anyone else does for a product or service. I might give a tip or do something else for salespeople or vendors, in addition to buying products at a good price. But what happens to the money I've kept by negotiating well is my business. What happens to the money I spend becomes the other person's business.

Likewise, I expect to pay my share of taxes (even though I realize a portion of them is going to be misspent). But I won't hand over any more taxes than I legally have to. I'll fight to keep what's mine, and I'll take advantage of every legal measure available to avoid paying more than I have to.

Speaking of Taxes

If you accept your real-estate tax assessment at face value, you might have a leak in your wallet. Track your taxes, so you have a history of what your taxes have been and what you've paid. And remember, people, including tax assessors and clerks, make mistakes. Appeal if you think you have a reasonable case.

We've appealed many times, when the potential reduction we thought valid was worth the cost and effort. In the negotiation, we have to consider what we'd like to get, what we can reasonably expect, and what we actually get. If we believe we should have 12 percent knocked off our taxes, but we get a reduction of only 7 percent, do we accept the adjustment? Yes, if a cost-benefit analysis shows the additional 5 percent would cost too much in attorney fees and if getting it back would take too long.

Sometimes we might contest a decision even if the process isn't cost effective, because the principle of the issue is at stake.

Managing Hard Times

We all are subject to economic downturns. If you keep your costs at the level you can afford during your periods of lowest income, staying out of financial difficulty will be easier. You must build your cash reserves for just such times. During the economic downturn of 1981, I lost, on paper, $1,000 a day, but we used our cash reserves to continue making loan payments. An accountant can work out what the actual reserves should be for your business.

It is important to consider, in advance of a crisis, your financial options. For example, you may be able to sell assets, such as buildings, then lease them back. A drastic measure, true, but better than losing everything. And don't overlook life insurance policies, against which you can borrow if the need arises.

Amazingly enough, one of the best sources of funding can be the tax system. We had been successful enough until the 1981 recession to have paid taxes every year, so we were able to reduce our cash outlay by avoiding estimated taxes in 1981. We also were able to take a tax loss for the year and get back money we had already paid.

We took jobs we ordinarily would have turned down, some minimally profitable, anything to keep the shop busy. We survived without laying off any employee. In other words, we retained our most important assets.

Banks and Bankers

Financial institutions use free checking accounts and other perks to attract you, but such baits distract you from the real issues. Your first concern should be the services you really need. For example, if you are doing international business, you need an international bank.

Are you an important customer to your bank, or can you become one? You may have to go to a smaller bank to become a more important customer. If possible, you want to be a big fish in a small pond. Ideally, you want to be among the 20 percent of the bank's largest clients. Find a bank of adequate size that will value you as a client.

Generally, the smallest bank that can service your business probably is going to do a better job for you than a big bank that offers a lot of services you don't need. The big bank has a large pool of customers; the little bank has to be more competitive and more attentive.

The Good Banking Customer

Whatever size customer you are, if you're a good customer, you have something to offer a bank. A good customer is one whose accounts are not costly to manage. You don't overdraw your checking account, you have a good credit rating, and you request reasonable loans and provide reasonable collateral. You consider your business from the banker's point of view.

Bankers look favorably upon good mortgage assets. The person who rents an office and computers to produce a software program, which is poor collateral, isn't going to get as far as the person who can say: "I have a building. I have machinery. I have inventory. I have a trained work force. I have a history of 25 years of solid cash flow and internally generated capital for growth."

The good condition of your premises is an asset. One of the first things Dun & Bradstreet representatives note in reviewing a business is whether its premises are clean and orderly. In short, does your business make a good presentation?

Bankers like to be proud of their clientele; they don't want to read about you in the newspaper because of problems. It is an advantage to say your business is respectable, that it isn't a "sin" business, such as a porn shop.

Get What You Deserve

A good customer deserves good service. Figure out your best selling points, the hidden value of your particular circumstances, then look for a bank that will customize a program for you from which you both can benefit.

Don't think you always have to accept the bank's offer. You won't know what terms you can get until you try. Arm yourself with the facts and assert yourself. Design a report showing your value to your bank — and don't be afraid to take it to another bank.

I want a banking relationship that takes into account the uniqueness of my business. We build a lot of expensive machinery, and we have costs from the moment we start gathering information to quote a job. We want to start recovering those costs as soon as possible, so we usually negotiate down payments on jobs that are custom-engineered.

We usually negotiate for receiving project payments in thirds: one-third initially; one-third when the project is half completed; the last third at completion. This way, we use the customer's money, rather than borrow the cash and thereby increase the overhead of the project. We don't have to borrow funds to capitalize their project, and we can pass that savings along to them.

We wanted a bank that would give us a line of credit we could bring into play as we needed it, rather than loan us a specific amount of money for a specific amount of time. Then, when we received these down payments, we could pay off our line of credit, instead of getting minimal interest on a savings account in which we deposited the down payments, while we were paying back a loan at 8 percent, or more, on a schedule.

We wanted to be able to pay off our loans irregularly, because we were getting these payments irregularly. We explained our idea to three banks. When we heard excuses like, "Our computer won't allow us to do that," we knew they weren't interested.

The bank that finally accommodated our request has benefited along with us. Our cash flow is about 50 percent more than when we started our partnership with the bank, so the bank's balance has grown with our deposits. Agreeing to that one request was like getting a customer one and a half times bigger over that period than we were initially. In addition, we have saved thousands of dollars in loan interest over the years that we have been with the bank. It has been a win-win situation.

Make Your Banker Compete for Your Business

You're aware of the market's competitive nature, but you may have to draw your banker's attention to it – nicely, of course. When I analyzed the sources of borrowed cash for our company, I found the bank we were using at the time accounted for less than 25 percent of our loans.
In addition, we were getting better deals from other sources, such as equipment manufacturers with lease-purchase programs. Meanwhile, the bank was getting the value of the flow of all our money through its institution.

I took this analysis with me to the bank and pointed out that the bank was not doing enough for a good customer. For the amount of money we were depositing, I thought the bank should be more competitive and should loan more money to our company. And as our account balances increased, I reasoned that we deserved larger loans, because, in actuality, we were borrowing back our own money.

In short, I thought, with all the money I was providing the bank, I should be getting a better deal. I offered to guarantee a balance of a certain size in my account, in return for which I wanted to be able to borrow more money. As a result of our discussion, the bank did work harder on the situation. It's up to us, the bank's customers, to point out our value to them. Since then, I keep close track of whether my bank's participation in our relationship is in parity with mine.

While negotiating with your banker, keep looking for other external cash sources. Use them as benchmarks with your banker. When you get a better deal from someone else, keep a record of what you should have gotten from your banker, so next time you can use the competitive nature of the marketplace to your benefit.

When I refinanced our house, the bank declined the opportunity, and I made the loan with another institution. The next time I negotiate with my banker, I will tell him he lost my business and why, hoping it encourages him to be more competitive in the future.

Working with Bankers

When I bought the NC punch press, which cost nearly three times what all my other machinery collectively was worth, I learned some important lessons about working with my banker.

First of all, keeping him informed all along as I developed my business helped smooth the way for a loan request that at first seemed outrageous and out of the question.

Second, keeping good records, including a financial statement, helped me prove I was capable of turning capital investments into profit.

Third, and perhaps most important, making a thorough presentation helped me convince my banker the loan I was asking for was worth the risk. I prepared well: I knew what I wanted and I could explain why I wanted it. I was efficient in my presentation and, to support my argument, I used collateral materials – pictures, graphs, and written descriptions my banker could hold in his hands, read, and file.

Bankers deal with all kinds of businesses. It's up to you to educate your banker about your company. If you're seeking a loan, you have to show why you aren't a serious risk and why the loan will be good for your business.

The True Value of Your Business

The real worth of anything is not what you pay for it; the real worth is what you get when you liquidate it. With few exceptions, things do not bring as much at resale as what is paid for them.

Depreciation usually reduces value immediately. Then, there are the ongoing costs of ownership, even if an item isn't used often: maintenance, space, insurance, heating and air conditioning, even taxation on personal goods, in some places. When an item is no longer needed or wanted, what is it worth? Only what it will bring on the market.

And don't assume all the components of a business are worth as much to a prospective buyer as they are to the would-be seller. Be careful about putting too strong a stamp of personal identity on your company. Some factors peculiar to the owner's interests may be as useful to someone else as a flashlight on a sunny day.

Say, for example, you enjoy going to Seattle, where you establish a satellite office and write off some of your expenses when you visit there. A potential buyer of your company with no interest in going to Seattle probably wouldn't consider that office an asset in your company's valuation.

In short, when you evaluate your business, consider it from a potential buyer's perspective. (See "Evaluating a Business" in chapter 2, "Acquiring a Business.")

Chapter 10
The Marketplace

As Dad expanded his farm interests, he began to do custom grain separation for farmers, before threshing machines had better sieves. Using separation equipment, we were able to remove the weed seeds from the bulk seed so it was pure enough for planting. We also produced and sold our own state-certified vetch seed. Vetch, a perennial, rejuvenates the nitrogen in the soil. The state certifies the quality of the seed. For several years we were Nebraska's largest certified vetch grower.

This kind of work required a big granary, a spiral separator, a fanning mill, and a scale, as well as shovels, bags, thread, labels, and certification seals. Mom and I ran the equipment all day, while Dad worked in the fields. The grain dropped through overhead bins into the separator. We scooped the grain into the fanning mill, then attached the sacks to the mill and filled them with pure grain seeds. Then we sewed the bags closed and put our "Certified" seal and tags on them. We always were racing the clock to fill an order.

Certified-grain sales represented a step beyond growing crops for sale. They represented a value-added process that commanded a higher unit price. With some additional equipment, we were able to get a higher income per bushel of grain. Thus, we were rewarded with a higher return on our farm investments.

Markets

The return on investments is a prime consideration in looking at markets. When I bought my manufacturing company, our markets included industrial customers, who wanted custom-built projects, as well as street customers, walk-ins who brought us their broken lawn equipment, snow blowers, tractors, and other small equipment to fix or who came to us to buy metal for their own projects. One employee took care of the walk-in business.

Analyzing our situation, I could see the walk-in customers weren't making us any money. Rather, each month they were costing us a lot in lost productivity, because our retail employee's time, about 25 hours a week, otherwise could have been spent on bigger and more lucrative projects of our industrial market. Put another way, cheap jobs and small sales that displace high-dollar projects will reduce cash flow and profit.

In our case, we couldn't invoice the big project on the shop floor as soon because we were welding somebody's lawnmower rather than completing the industrial work. Additionally, I realized our small customers were not repeat customers.

Then and there I decided to opt out of the walk-in market, quit repairing small equipment, and focus on industrial projects. We stopped selling small batches of materials to individuals and turned, instead, to focusing on the sale of raw materials to the industrial market.

As I analyzed all the jobs we had been doing, I considered the ratio of labor costs to material costs. Jobs with a ratio of one to one or less weren't worth our while, because labor costs don't get the mark-up in price material costs get. So I set a goal ratio of one to six. That is, for every dollar's worth of labor I'd sell, I wanted to sell at least $6 in materials.

For us, the only way I could see to do that was to develop the metals distribution side of our business. Rather than creating and selling fabricated metal products, this side only sells metals in stock sizes or cut to order. What once was a minimal walk-in sales business became a significant part of our growth. The distribution component of our business now stands on its own, only because of the strategic decision to identify and define the value of selling to the existing marketplace.

Name Your Business

When I bought the company, the only change I made in the name was from "company" to "corporation." Customers already recognized the original name, and that recognition and continuity were worth a lot in marketing dollars.

If you change the name, your customers have to learn about your company all over again. With a name change, you indicate other changes may be occurring, and people are cautious about changes where their money is concerned. A new name requires further explanation and a bigger budget to explain it. In the long run, you have set up another hurdle to overcome as you try to grow the business.

Besides identification, a name should double as a marketing tool. If you must rename your company or if you are starting a business, choose a name that explains something about the company to potential customers. Don't contrive a word that has no meaning to the marketplace. Minimize the explaining you have to do. You want potential customers to figure out quickly what it is your company can do for them. Simple is good; the less confusion, the better.

Place Your Business

Obviously, there are numerous issues to consider when deciding where to locate your company. Having access to the services your business requires, the kinds of employees you need, especially if they're specialists, and the kinds of inventory you require is vital. Zoning laws have to be considered.

For some businesses, fast food, say, traffic is everything. Suppose I am considering opening a hamburger stand. I would research the flow and the demographics of the neighborhood, the amount of expendable income spent on fast food, all the pertinent details. Then, I'd locate near McDonald's! Even if they made a mistake in their research, the flow of traffic will seek out McDonald's.

But not all businesses need or even want to be in the flow. Our original building was in the center of town on a busy street, where we constantly were in the public eye. Seeing us when they drove by, consumers would stop in and ask us to weld their broken lawnmowers and barbecue grills. We wasted much of our time directing them to other shops that did that kind of work.

Additionally, getting big trucks to our loading docks was difficult. One machine we built was so big we had to roll it on a wheeled pallet through the double doors of my office and into the street, where I had people out with flashing lights to block traffic, so we could load the machine onto a semi. All this at five in the morning before traffic got heavy.

So for me, being too convenient to consumers and too inconvenient for trucks was bad. I found an industrial park that had all the services and space I need, a place out of the public eye, a place where I'm not going to get crosswise with home dwellers in a residential area, a place where I'm welcome. And of course, there's the issue of taxes. Because our new location was outside the city limits, we saved 6 percent on the cost of our construction materials by avoiding sales taxes.

Position Yourself

I once saw a sign in a print shop that read: Price – Quality – Delivery – Pick two.

There you have it – the three basics of service. The sign says you get to pick only two of the basics. If you want the best price and the best delivery time, according to this sign, the quality may be less than desired. If you want the best quality and you want it within your time frame, then you're going to have to pay more.

We want to be known for high quality. That was one of our marketing decisions. Even if we weren't making a profit on a project, we wouldn't want to risk our reputation by lowering our quality. So for any job, we make adjustments only in price and delivery.

Caution: Market Survey

Be wary of market surveys. Do you know who sponsored the survey and what their bias is? Do you know what questions were asked and of whom they were asked to get the reported results?

Customers

Once you define your market, your basic concerns are where to find customers and what to sell them. If you approach the process systematically, you may have an easier time.

Looking for Sales

A simple matrix defines the dynamics of prospecting for business:

- Old customer – old product
- Old customer – new product
- New customer – old product
- New customer – new product

The best source of business is old – that is, regular – customers (preferably old, good customers). These people are familiar to you; you are familiar to them. You know what they need and expect. They've come to trust you and you, them. The easiest sell is an old product, something familiar, to an old customer. The second easiest sell is a new product to an old customer. Again, that customer trusts you, so he's willing to take a chance on something unfamiliar you want to sell him.

Selling an old product to a new customer is harder. The product is tried and true, but the customer doesn't know what to expect from you. And, naturally, the most difficult sell is a new product to a new customer. Everything is an unknown. Why should he trust you?

I remember an experience at an airport where my wife and I had just landed our small plane. Noncommercial aircraft use a for-profit flight-based operator (FBO) for services. We asked for fuel when we rolled up and shut down the engine, but the attendant at the FBO responded rudely and mumbled his answers. He acted as if he didn't care whether we did business with him or not.

In short, he didn't gain our trust, and we were unhappy with his service. I wasn't sure whether he could, even would, fill the tanks correctly.

We were new customers to him, and he was selling us an old product. Easy enough, but had we any choice about the matter, we'd have gone elsewhere. Instead, we monitored him more carefully than usual, watching to make sure that he filled our tanks with 100 low-lead fuel, instead of jet fuel, that he topped the tanks properly and closed the filler caps, that he didn't leave spills on the wing that would harm the paint. He didn't act like a professional, and we weren't sure how well he could do his job.

The first concern for a businessperson is to gain the confidence of the customer. We all have certain hopeful notions of people and settings, and we are more comfortable when our expectations are met; it makes the unknown seem more familiar to us. As you satisfy your customers' needs, consider how you also can fulfill their expectations. Do everything your good clients have a right to expect from you, operationally and professionally.

Presenting a pleasant demeanor that inspires trust rather than causes people to put up their guard is an important element. I'm talking not only about you as you meet with customers but also about your receptionist, who, with just a tone of voice in one brief encounter, can encourage business or drive it away. Hire a receptionist who puts people at ease.

Especially, make sure your business premises are clean and organized, your delivery trucks clean and professional looking. First impressions can make the difference between a sale and second thoughts.

Research Your Sales Calls

Before you drop in on potential customers, do your research. Learn something about their business. You don't want to ask inappropriate questions and earn a reputation for being silly. More important, you want to determine the likelihood of their buying your products, so you don't waste their time or yours.

You also want to know whether they are likely to be good customers. That is, can they pay, and will they pay on time? Are they decent to their vendors, or do they have a reputation for being problem buyers? Consider the guy who would order a die from a company,

COD, then refuse it when it arrived at his dock. The vendor would call, and he'd complain that the die wasn't just right and start negotiating for a lower price with the vendor, who had no use for the custom die.

Generally, it's the naive businesses just starting up that get taken by customers like that. Do your homework.

All Customers Are Not Equal

You don't need every customer. You don't even want every customer. You want valuable customers. So set your criteria for what a "good" customer is. Using those criteria, build up a good clientele, and take care of those customers the best way you know. Weed out troublesome customers.

The idea of choosing customers might sound a little unappreciative. After all, the general concept behind marketing and advertising programs is to attract more customers. But setting standards, even turning away those who don't measure up to your requirements, makes sense. It is neither audacious nor arrogant to have criteria against which you rate those with whom you do business. In fact, you probably already have some measurements, though you may not have consciously deliberated about them. Perhaps this discussion will prompt you to give more thought to your situation.

You have to be able to do the work within agreed-upon parameters. But other issues also arise when considering which business to accept. If you are successful enough to have customers competing for your time and expertise, how can you establish some order in the process? Let me answer by turning the tables for a moment and making you the customer.

Let's say you do $20,000 in business a year with a little shop. It's a large percentage of the shop's income. Along comes a one-time customer, and the little shop displaces the work you give it on a regular basis with the project of this one-time customer. Then, because the shop is so busy, you get charged overtime to have your regular work delivered on schedule.

In effect, you've just been "fined." And this vendor has treated you as if the amount of business you provide doesn't count for anything.

The "take-a-number" method of dealing with customers does a disservice to your best customers. Contrary to the ideal of a classless society, in the business world some customers should take precedence over others.

If you believe, as I do, that behaviors have consequences, then you readily can accept the notion that some customers should get a higher rating and others deserve to wait. The ones who give you a lot of business and who pay you promptly deserve preferential treatment over those who use your services only infrequently or whose lackadaisical payment methods make you work even harder to get the dollars you earn.

Rate Your Customers

We look at several criteria to determine, first, whether we accept the customer and, second, where the customer fits in our hierarchy of importance. After all, keeping the company alive is the underlying rationale for most decisions, so it follows we should rate our customers according to how valuable they are to our business.

Now, by "valuable" I don't mean just how much income they will provide us. Though that, of course, is an important factor, it isn't the only one. To ignore the other serious considerations is asking for trouble, maybe more trouble than the worth of a problem customer's account.

Establish a set of criteria so you can rank your customers, say, Class I through Class IV. We decide which customers have what priority by going through an analysis something like this:

- Will the customer pay us promptly?
- Can we do the work profitably?
- Will the job fit into our work flow, or will it disrupt ongoing projects for our other important customers?
- Will the job use the whole hive or just one cup of honey – in other words, more rather than less of the company's capital investment?
- What is the ratio of labor to materials?
- Is this a one-time project?

- Does the customer think of us as a resource who can help him out of trouble or as someone to blame if something goes wrong with his project on which we're working?

Those companies for which we get the most satisfactory answers are our Class I customers. Now let's look at those issues one by one.

PROMPT PAYMENT – Before we agree to do a job, we check a potential customer's credit rating through a service to which we subscribe that lists companies' financial strength and payment ability. A less-than-perfect credit rating doesn't necessarily mean we will turn down a customer, but it alerts us to pay closer attention to the customer's line of credit with us and to the schedule and method of payments.

PROFITABLE PROJECTS – Obviously, we couldn't stay in business if we gave away our services or our products. So we look at whether the jobs we already have done for the customer have been consistently profitable. Next, we evaluate how profitable the requested project is likely to be.

These two considerations include how difficult the customer is after the sale. Follow-up consultations, adjustments, reworks, and training are part of the overhead of a job. We try to anticipate them, so we can build them into the pricing equation. But those follow-ups the customer unexpectedly springs on us erode the bottom line, and they cause sticky negotiations and sometimes hard feelings.

GOING WITH THE FLOW – Any job that doesn't fit into our normal flow of work gets a red flag. For example, a customer might want us to come out on a Saturday or a Sunday to work on a job that otherwise requires shutting down the production line. Or another project might cause scheduling problems and generate unnecessary overtime for our employees. Or it might tie up time and employees to the detriment of our other customers.

THE WHOLE HIVE – The more of my capital investment I use to service a customer, the better my return on that investment. If I have a hundred machines but take on a project that uses only 50 of them, then half of my investment is sitting idle.

Look at the situation another way: The cost of machinery is amortized over several projects, so a machine or an investment unused is wasted capacity. You'd get the same rate of return if you plunked your savings into a no-interest account.

THE RATIO OF LABOR TO MATERIALS – The garage that services your car gets a higher markup on the oil and the filter than it does on the time an employee spends changing your oil. So, if you buy your oil at a discount house, is your mechanic going to be ecstatic about having you as a customer? Never. I determined early on that the bottom line benefited most if I sell as much material per hour of labor as I can.

REPEAT BUSINESS – How frequently a customer comes to us is a big factor in deciding whether or not to take on a job. For instance, sometimes a company coming into town to put up a new plant will come to us for a quick turnaround on a must-have job. The company needs us only for this one isolated situation, so we know we aren't going to be a regular vendor to them. We couldn't justify displacing a regular customer's work for a construction "emergency" requested by someone we're never going to see again.

THE CUSTOMER'S VIEW OF US – Occasionally, a company representative whose project is in trouble will try to pass the blame to the vendor, who is beyond the wrath of the rep's supervisor inside the company. But we would much rather deal with someone who, instead, thinks of us as a team member on whom he can call to get him out of a crunch. Just human nature, I suppose, but it counts in our rating system.

Sometimes the replacement of just one person in a company can alter our whole relationship with the company as a customer. We have moved a customer up or down our ranking system because the company switched our contact person or changed its business philosophy.

We constantly monitor the value of the business our customers do with us. If we suspect a customer's standing with us might have changed, we'll do an annual evaluation and look at the history of the account: every job we've done for that company, the profit ratios, how much money we've made, how many hours in a year we've spent with the company, how much material and labor we've sold them. The customer may move up or down the ranks, depending upon the results of the analysis.

The Pareto Principle

Are you familiar with the Pareto Principle? Also called the "80:20 Rule," it originally was developed by Vilfredo Pareto, an Italian economist, to describe the phenomenon that about 80 percent of wealth in most countries is controlled by about 20 percent of the people.

Others have extrapolated his ratio, especially applicable to management issues, to describe the relationship between output and input. For example, 80 percent of the revenue comes from 20 percent of the projects, or 80 percent of the problems are caused by 20 percent of the employees. The generalization fits countless situations.

Apply the 80:20 rule to your client base. How many clients supply 80 percent of your revenue? Who are they? You are in a precarious position if most of your revenue comes from only a few clients. Just one "gorilla," one large customer, who betrays you, can ruin your company.

Many years ago, I heard about a situation in which a large national company offered some small companies a lot of business to produce items the large company sold. The purchasing agent offered a blanket order for their products if they would increase their capital equipment to meet the increase in production.

That sounded like a good deal to those small-business owners. With a bigger order than they'd ever had, they invested a lot of money in equipment, employees, and other overhead costs. Initially they had a year's contract to make the products.

Everything seemed great, except there were penalties if the little companies didn't produce the items by a certain time, and the big company nit-picked the quality. There were tight controls over servicing that account for this premier customer.

Further, the little companies probably had to let slide their service to other customers assumed to be less valuable. The little companies had made a huge investment, with little profit on it at that stage, because all the initial costs were not a normal part of production.

Then the big company changed its sales strategy. It wanted the small companies to make changes in the items they were producing and then reduced the size of its order. Still the biggest customer, the gorilla was beating his chest and making threatening gestures.

There was little the small companies could do. Many went bankrupt or were bought up by the big company. The managers had put themselves into a position in which they had no flexibility about decisions that affected the welfare of their companies. They lost control. Then, they lost their companies.

Evaluate your client list annually. Look at it as you do your financial investment portfolio. You wouldn't sink a large portion of your wealth into one stock, at least not if you want to limit your risk.

In reality, your factory, your employees, and your other resources are an investment, and you should assess what percentage of those resources you allot to a single client. Consider how much of your capital investment is going to be offset by any one client, and balance your client portfolio so no client becomes a gorilla in your company.

The Customer Is Not Always Right

With these concerns fresh in your mind, know that the customer is not always right. Still, the customer always thinks he's right. Some customers even know they're not right, but they think they'll get more out of you if they're difficult. And, of course, some simply like to throw their weight around, like the one who ignored our "No Smoking" sign and lit up a cigar. When I pointed out the sign, he said, "But I'm a customer." "These are my employees," I replied, "and none of them likes cigar smoke." He put out the cigar.

While I was working for another metals company, I dealt with a difficult man who ran a small division of a big company that did a lot of work with us. Every job he gave us was a rush job, and he expected it to be at the best price. His own people laughed at him. They said he was the only guy who could lose money on a cost-plus job, because he would go out and get five price estimates on a 2-x-4-foot wood stud.

I was the only nonfamily person taking work orders in this family-owned company for which I worked, and I was the lowest man on the totem pole. Nobody else liked the bully any more than I did, so I always ended up dealing with him.

One time he wanted some metal plates cut for an overhang on a building. I went out to the site to take measurements. The day was cold and windy, and I had to stand on a 12-foot ladder to measure all the openings underneath the overhang. "Mr. Nasty" didn't even offer to help.

When I finished the job, which took an hour and a half, he handed me a piece of paper with all the measurements on it and laughed. "I just wanted to see if your measurements were the same as mine," he said. In the time it took me to measure for those parts, I could have had all the pieces cut and had time left over to recut any that were wrong.

I was mad, but I couldn't say anything to him, because, working for somebody else, I was in no position to chastise him.

I went home. At two o'clock the next morning, I was still awake and still mad. Then I thought: Parks, you know what he's good for? He's good for making you appreciate how wonderful your other customers are, because they don't do that to you. They're considerate and friendly, and you get a good feeling of accomplishment by helping them.

This bully taught me two things. One lesson was to cherish decent customers. The second was to protect my employees from bad customers.

Now that I run my own company, I tell my people, "You don't ever have to take bad behavior from customers. If they're making your life miserable, let's discuss the issues." We then make a decision about that customer, and it may be that we don't want to do work for him anymore. There have been times when vendors have had to take abuse from customers. Today we don't have to.

At times, you may need to deal directly with a customer to correct a difficult situation, but don't let customers sidestep your salespeople and come to you. It demoralizes your sales staff. When a customer of ours jumped across the whole system to get to me, I fixed his problem, but I told the salesman not to take another order from him. The salesman had been doing a good job and I had worked hand in hand with him. Nevertheless, the customer thought I would give him a better deal. He was more trouble than he was worth. Let your sales staff handle their customers.

When is a bad customer too bad? In addition to extreme rudeness or violating your system, another consideration is whether the customer is disrupting your other business too much. If a demanding customer causes so much turmoil he affects your ability to service your other customers, or if he has a negative effect on your employees, then that customer is no good for your company.

Scrutinize the Business You're Offered

When you analyze a prospective job, start with the three basics of service: quality, price, and delivery. Can I provide this customer with what he wants, with the quality he wants, within a price range he is willing to pay, within the time frame he wants it? Of course, all of these issues are fluid, and when you're negotiating a project, you're going to pick up on which is most important to your customer.

If he's looking for bottom dollar, for example, but you're not a bottom-dollar shop, or you don't have an advantage in machinery to do the project more cheaply than your competitor, say no. If the delivery date is unreasonable for you, say no.

If you can't meet the expectations of the customer, decline the request, because the chance for success is limited. And any future chance for success with that customer will be destroyed – not to mention your reputation damaged – if you make promises you can't keep.

Why the Sudden Rush?

Considering how hard it is to find good customers, a sudden surge of business might seem like a godsend. But I'm telling you to be wary if customers start beating down your door to get your product. It may not be the opportunity it looks like.

Figure out why it's happening. Perhaps your prices are too low, compared with the rest of the marketplace. Perhaps there is a shortage in the market for what you're selling.

In times when certain metal goods were in short supply, people who weren't my regular customers suddenly wanted to do business with me, because I happened to have those goods in stock. If I couldn't service my regular customers because I couldn't replace that inventory during the shortage of goods, if I had to replace it at a higher price, and if I were forced to pass that cost on to my faithful, long-term customers, I would have paid more in the long run.

Keep the bigger picture in mind when you consider windfall "opportunities." Evaluate their potential effect on your regular customers.

You may have a sudden surge of traffic because another supplier went out of business. Consider why it happened before you fill that void. Maybe the supplier went under because such jobs are too competitive and the customer was used to low prices and was spoiled. Then you're looking at another horse with a bad set of teeth.

Maybe a new government regulation is forcing new requirements on the potential customers. Aha! This could be a good horse, a real opportunity. Or, it could be another distraction that displaces your regular customers.

Have a clear idea of who you are and what you are willing to do in the marketplace. Often, so-called "opportunities" have needs peripheral to what you do well, what you are experienced at, what you are prepared to do at the time, or what the marketplace is willing to do. Before you take a job, analyze whether it suits your market position.

Say No to Bad Business

When considering any business opportunity, whether an order, a new product, or an expansion, look at it from as many angles as you can. If a project looks too good to be true, it may be. Be extra cautious.

Several years ago, the Postmaster General's office put out a bid request for a $7-million project. We were interested, and a representative from Washington, visiting us to see if we were qualified to do the job, approved us. In preparing the bid, I called her with five questions about specifications we needed to know. I received no answer to them, so we submitted a bid based only on the information we did have.

The U.S. Postal Service gave the job to a company whose bid was $1 million lower. But the company failed, according to the Postal Service representative, who then offered us the project. Although it could have been a profitable project for us, I remembered that the representative who visited us to check on our capability was a bureaucrat with no manufacturing experience. She hadn't a clue about what to look for. Uncomfortable with the situation, I decided to do some sleuthing before I accepted the project.

I'm glad I did. When I called the owner of the rejected company to ask what had happened, he told me about the problems he'd had with the Postal Service representatives. The standards and criteria were vague, he said. Trying to get the information from the bureaucrats in Washington had proved fruitless, because they themselves didn't know the specifics of the project. The Postal Service refused his work, leaving him to foot the bill for thousands of dollars in special-order materials.

I called our contact at the Washington office again to ask for specification on the issues for which the failed contractor had been rejected. After five days, I hadn't received an answer, so I called again. When I questioned her about why she hadn't called me back, her reply was, "My boss said, 'Why does he want to know that?'"

We had spent a month getting the bid ready on that job, lost the job, and gotten it back. Then I thought, why should I risk my business when someone won't answer five simple questions for me about issues that have proven costly to the previous vendor? And they were just technical questions that would have made the specifications clear for both us and the Postal Service.

I realized we were being set up to fail, just as the other company did. So I refused the job, though it looked very profitable on paper.

Look carefully at your customers and their projects. The wrong job or a job from the wrong customer could be a disastrous venture. Be willing to decline if the numbers don't work out or if something about the project makes you uneasy.

Dirty Birds

A bird in the hand isn't necessarily worth two in the bush. The bird in your hand might be a dirty bird – a customer with a credit risk, an unreasonably short delivery deadline, too small a profit. If you're holding a dirty bird when a dove comes along, you have missed a better opportunity. You've committed the company to producing that order, and you've displaced a good order.

Granted, when the marketplace is tight and there are fewer projects available, you have to adjust your criteria. But don't resort to taking projects from problem customers until you've exhausted the possibilities of your top clients.

Watch the horizon, not your toes. Your scouts – your salespeople – can help you see what the marketplace is offering, or will be offering:

"X Company is doing a plant expansion in Michigan. We've quoted 15 projects for them. They don't have any money in the budget right now, but in 30 days, when the new budget is released, they're going to let those projects. We should wait for them."

If we know the prospects are out there, we'd rather paint the shop and fix equipment, waiting for them, than take a job in the meantime from a problem customer whose project will tie up our shop. There are times when it's better to do nothing and to keep the door open for opportunity than to take on a marginal project that displaces a better one.

Offset Risk with Profit

Balancing your client portfolio means analyzing the risk of doing business with each client. Everything you do, every order you take, has a ratio of risk to return. The question to ask is: How much return will I get for the risk I have to take?

Financially, you can play it as safe as possible and put all your money into a safe-deposit box at the bank, or you can take measured risks of varying degrees and invest your money in anything from U.S. Treasury bills to junk bonds. By the same token, you can take only "guaranteed" orders in your business. If you are smarter, you will allot a percentage of your business to higher-risk accounts. As in financial investments, the higher the risk, usually, the greater the return.

For instance, the steel-distribution business during the 1970s was so competitive that a high percentage of the profits came from businesses with high credit risk. They didn't get the best price because the pool of businesses servicing such accounts was smaller. The companies dealing with these high-risk businesses charged more, so the companies' profit margins were greater. Their rate of return was better.

It is reasonable to have a certain amount of riskier business, but keep the risk in mind when you set your profit. The smaller the profit margin, the greater the effect of failure of payment. If your profit margin is 10 percent, you have to sell that same-size order 10 times to recoup the lost payment. If you have a profit margin of 30 percent, you have to sell that same-size order three and a third times to recoup it if the invoice isn't paid.

Business can be riskier for many reasons. An order may require a higher quality than your company usually provides. If you take it but charge the regular price, your margins will be less, because the quality considerations will cost you more. If the time frame in which you have to produce is short, you probably will have higher costs. That's because you'll likely have overtime and your suppliers may have overtime, if they have to provide products to you within a shorter time frame.

In addition, the pool of suppliers who can meet your demands for higher quality may be smaller. And if marketplace competition forces you to take an order with a lower profit margin, you have no cushion for any increased risk.

If a customer's request is out of the ordinary, and particularly if you are concerned about ability to pay or about profit margin, scrutinize the request with squinty eyes and consider carefully whether you even want the business. At the least, I would insist on a high profit margin from someone who has a poor pay history. I would settle for a lower profit margin from a customer whose pay history is better.

One of the compelling reasons to accept such a job would be a full workforce and empty workspace. In that situation, generally, I'd give something to get that book of business, were I compelled. I might be willing to reduce the price, for example. However, I would not give extended terms.

The worst thing you can do is get into a situation where a high-risk client owes you, not only because it takes so much more business just to make up for what you have lost if he doesn't pay, but also because of the overhead of trying to recoup the debt – attorneys' fees, court costs, and so forth. And I haven't even computed into the equation the other opportunities lost while you're dealing with the delinquent.

Establish Parity

As a business, our job is to take care of all our customers. But our best customers receive priority for all the reasons I've described. If we're going to protect our company, a request from a customer with lower standing requires extra consideration.

To accept a less desirable project requires we offset whatever makes it less desirable. We try to give it parity with more desirable projects by adjusting the variables, such as payment methods, scheduling or, commonly, profit margin. For example, we will demand payment up front from a customer with a bad pay history. Or we might take a less desirable job if we can work on it after we've finished all our other projects.

Because we've set up our operation to draw the kind of business most beneficial to us, an undesirable job probably doesn't fit into our normal costing system. We would have to customize even that part of the process. In addition, we generally can't add value to goods at the same rate on work outside the normal production process as we can on regular work. And of course, added value is where the profit is.

The question becomes: What extra markup must we have on this job to say we're willing to do it? Even twice the normal return wouldn't induce us to take some jobs.

Train Your Customers

Just as all customers are not equal, so all jobs are not equal. Some are drudgery, others pleasant. Some are difficult, others easy. Some have a narrow profit margin, others are better for the bottom line. You aren't going to get the best jobs all the time, but you also shouldn't get only the worst jobs from a customer.

If you're willing to take all the crummy jobs, then that's what a customer is going to give you, because peddling an unpleasant project to vendors is more difficult than peddling a good one. For employee morale – and the long-term good of your company – try to strike a balance. Accept some of the drudgery jobs, if you're well rewarded economically for them (in which case you've brought them into parity with the better ones), but try to persuade your customers to send some of their better jobs your way now and then as a reward.

If you're getting only the hard, unpleasant jobs from a company, rethink the relationship. You may decide not to pursue that customer as ardently, perhaps not bending over backwards to meet their delivery dates. After all, that company isn't a Class I customer.

Control Credit

Slow-paying customers siphon off your profits by taking up the time your employees could be spending on other things. One way to protect yourself from them is to establish a strict credit policy. Banks will set up a credit line to loan a family $20,000 as a personal loan. But we loan companies that kind of money, and much more, all the time: accounts receivable are *loans*.

Companies without a credit policy are allowing their customers, good and bad, to set their credit policy for them. Those companies then have to take only what they can get from such customers. We don't do that. We set the credit policy for our customers.

A friend of mine couldn't collect on a bill of more than $800 that a company owed him. He didn't have a policy; he just got mad. We said we'd do business with this company, but we required half the payment down at the start of the project and the other half on delivery.

In the period of time my friend was trying to collect his $800, we did about $120,000 worth of business with that company. It was because we had a tough credit program that we took the business and got paid.

Always, knowing how a customer pays is part of our discussions about any project. That criterion determines how aggressively we will go after the work and how competitive we'll be.

Our credit policy is complex. We sit down in committee and decide what our credit line is for a customer, just like a bank would do. We usually know ahead of time a customer could be slow to pay, because we've checked with our credit-rating service. We flag problem accounts, and we make notes of what we will and will not do.

When an account is overdue, the computer flashes a notice, and employees trained to handle slow-paying customers start making phone calls. Then we remember that customer, and we try not to get caught again.

Customers are not always right, but they are customers and, of course, you want to preserve your relationships with them, if possible. But set limits on credit for each customer. Keep track of the age of the account and of orders in place. If a customer is seriously overdue, the shop should not be producing more debt by continuing to work on the project.

Vendors

The most fundamental way to evaluate a vendor is to look at your own considerations first. Do you care most about price, quality, or delivery?

But consider, too, the virtues of a good vendor. A good vendor is one who supplies reliable products competitively priced. The vendor's shipping department rarely makes mistakes. Your order is packaged so well that it arrives in its original condition on time. The vendor's accounts-receivable department bills you accurately and sends the bill in time for you to get your discounts when you pay it. And if you have a problem, you can talk to a representative, who will make sure your problem is resolved to your satisfaction.

Obviously, it's up to you to investigate the reputation of vendors before you do business with them. Talk to other businesses. Once you place an order, follow up on the processing. Look at every aspect of the order and consider how well it was fulfilled. Was the order written correctly? Did the vendor package the shipment adequately? Is the bill correct? Did the vendor stand behind the product?

Those are the criteria and they are simple ones but, instead, many people think price is the only consideration. Bottom dollar doesn't always indicate the best vendor or lowest overall cost. You might get something for a dollar cheaper, then spend a lot more because the order arrived late and in bad shape. You had to fix it yourself, then go back and bill the vendor for rework. The headache alone isn't worth the dollar, let alone the overhead of the repair.

And if you have resourceful employees, they may fix something that arrives in bad shape without saying anything to anybody. Then you wonder why the price of the job is up, because "straightening out something" wasn't considered in the bid for that job. So watch your own people, too. Ask them whether the vendors are doing what they're supposed to do.

How to Keep Your Vendors Happy

We know what a good vendor looks like. Now, should you care about being a good customer? The answer will be obvious the next time you need a favor from one of your vendors, such as a quick turnaround or a best price.

The customer from Hell is one who increases the vendor's overhead by ordering the wrong thing, then returning it, for which the vendor has to reinventory and follow up on the paperwork. The customer from Hell squeals about the price, either before or after the sale. He tries to get a break by complaining about little things. Then, he is slow to pay or, worse, "forgets" to pay and forces the vendor to follow up with additional phone calls or paperwork.

I want my vendors to think highly of me. If I treat them right, when it comes down to a real competitive situation, I won't feel guilty about asking for a little break: "Look, I need 30 of these and this is a tight job. You have to sharpen your pencil on this one." If they look at my "Pay" record, and it's bad, what's in it for them to sharpen their pencils?

A good customer places orders right the first time, so there aren't a lot of returns. One way to make sure you avoid ordering wrong is to write down your order and review it before you place it. Second, a good customer pays promptly. Third, a good customer doesn't nitpick. Whining about little things might get you a small adjustment in price at the time, but it also will get you a big reputation for being difficult. Payback will come eventually.

Support Local Vendors

Do business with local vendors when you can; after all, they are part of your community. If you can get an item from a vendor elsewhere at a better deal, discuss the situation with your local vendor: "Look, I can buy this in Kansas City for less money, and it's just as good and I can get it just as quickly as I can get it from you, sometimes more quickly. But I'd rather do business with you. Can you do anything about your price or delivery?" Give your local vendor the opportunity to compete.

It's also good policy to use more than one source for the products you need. If your sole supplier goes out of business, or if that vendor can't get you all you need for a special order, you may have to scramble to find a substitute. You might even miss out on the job, because you couldn't find another source. Extend your business to several vendors.

Give your vendors as much time as possible to fulfill your order. Don't make everything a "Rush" job because it sat unattended on your desk. Save "Rush" orders for legitimate reasons, not self-made circumstances.

Running your business smoothly depends upon maintaining good relationships with your vendors. Take care of the good ones and make sure they have reason to appreciate you as a customer. You'll get the best service if you do.

Expand Your Pool

Purchasing requires never-ending research. Look at not only what your needs are today but also what your potential needs are. In addition to finding new products for old purposes, you also want to know about new sources for products. You want a bigger pool of competitors from which to choose. You want a bigger pool of quality.

When my old insurance company dropped us without warning, I didn't have to start from zero to find new coverage, because when I had insurance, I still met with insurance representatives who dropped by on cold sales calls. I collected their business cards and made a few notes on them. When I needed insurance, I immediately was able to pull names and start looking through a pre-screened pool of agents.

Don't Be Sold

When a salesperson comes to see you, what do you do? More to the point, what have you done? If you haven't prepared ahead of time, you are less likely to be in control of the outcome of the meeting, and you are in danger of being sold rather than buying.

You need a strategy. Now, you've heard that the best defense is a good offense. Here's one: Develop a list of simple questions, whether in your head or on paper, for the salesperson to answer. This way, rather than being on the defensive against baloney, you are on the offensive for information. Putting together that list will make you think for yourself about the products, before the salesperson gets the opportunity to try to direct your point of view.

Another reason for having a list of questions is that you can focus on facts rather than on what you might like to hear. Many a car is sold on the basis of a pretty paint job and sleek lines. A shiny chrome finish can distract us from what we really should be finding out. As you listen, ask yourself what is actually being said. Does it ring true? Consider, too, what isn't being said.

Having a list of questions ready will help you listen, because you will have an idea of the information you should get. A person simply writing down whatever a salesperson says is more likely to be swayed, more likely to be sold.

While in this meeting, note whether the salesperson asks about your business. If he doesn't know much about your company, he can't know how his product can help you, or even whether it will. He probably isn't looking out for your best interests. That's another reason to be on the defensive.

When I meet with salespeople, I even go so far as to throw concepts into my orientation about the company (information I know salespeople couldn't possibly know beforehand), to see if they'll ask a question. If they don't, I give up on them almost immediately, because I figure, if they're just pretending to understand me, they're probably not really listening, and I doubt they're concerned about what I need.

What's more, if they aren't learning about my business, they aren't learning how their product can help me. And if they don't know that, then what's the point of wasting time with them?

Another aspect of the defensive position is the "antischmooze play." First of all, remember that giving a salesperson permission to try to sell you something does not mean you agree to buy. You have no obligation to buy what someone is trying to sell you. Keep it that way. I don't like gifts or even a free lunch from a vendor, because it reduces my ability to remain a buyer, rather than someone to be sold to.

Lunch is a small price for a vendor to pay for your business. It could cost you a lot if it makes you feel obligated to buy something you didn't truly need or want or could have gotten elsewhere for much less.

Basics of Negotiating

When I was a sophomore in high school, I secretly wrote away for employment with a Yellowstone National Park concessionaire. I filled out an application and got back a letter describing the wages and the room and board. It sounded great to me. I wanted to get away from the farm.

Dad wouldn't let me take the job but, by showing him that letter, I was able to negotiate with him for a wage and at least some of the benefits the concessionaire was offering. He started paying me $30 a week for working 12 hours a day, and he let me use the shop oil for my car and fill up my gas tank out of the farm barrel.

I'd been doing a man's work since the age of nine. By bringing in the external pressure of that offer from an outsider, I had shown I was marketable. I finally started getting an income. Other farmers wanted me to work for them and, as their offers rose, I was able to improve my salary by negotiating with Dad. I began to have a little independence and some fun.

What Is Negotiation?

Interaction is negotiation. When a kid whines for a cookie, he's negotiating with his mom. When we reach for our wallet, we're doing business and negotiating. The way you walk into a store and say hello begins your negotiation with the salesperson. You immediately start setting the kind of relationship in which this deal will occur, even if it's just buying a cup of coffee.

Generally, doing business is a continuing series of negotiations. The best of them occur within longstanding relationships, and over the years give and take occurs in the context of that bigger picture.

The hardest negotiations are one-time deals with people you'll never see again.

The Lowest Form of Negotiation

Most people seem to have only rudimentary negotiating skills. They believe simply that competitive shopping and whining to their suppliers will get prices down. So they go out and get three bids and demand that the vendor match the lowest one. Or they complain and scowl and threaten and exhibit other mean behaviors.

Unfortunately, such nastiness works just well enough that people continue to use it, even where intimidation doesn't yield results – with bankers, for example, insurance underwriters, government representatives. But if you make people angry by trying to intimidate them, do you think they're going to look for ways to enhance their relationship with you? On the contrary, they're going to rid themselves of you, if they can.

You'll go much further by gathering information and making a compelling case for yourself.

Analyze the Situation

Before you start negotiating seriously, do your research. You might have bought the same brand of machine from the salesperson for the past 15 years, but if you haven't kept track of what that machine is going for on the market now, and if you don't have a good record of what you've paid before, you won't know how good a deal the salesperson is offering you.

Know what you want, but don't be inflexible. Instead, accommodate the circumstances of the negotiation. Be willing to wait. Analyze the environment of buying and selling.

Are you negotiating with someone who has the final say, or someone who has to get approval? Are you dealing with someone who's retiring soon or someone who's just getting started? A salesperson who has only a month to go might not be as likely to give you a good price on the expensive machine you're going to buy. With retirement looming, a bigger commission might be more enticing than staying on good terms with you.

On the other hand, a young salesperson who has a family to support might be more interested in establishing a long-term relationship with you so you become a source of frequent, even if smaller, commissions.

Know what's in the negotiation for the other person. How does that person benefit from the situation? If a computer company provides its sales force with an incentive to get a quantity of computers out into the field so they aren't on inventory at year's end, the salesperson might be more interested in the final tally of computers than in the money he essentially will give away in negotiation to get those computers out there.

Chapter 11
Consultants: Your
Team of Experts

In 1945, times were bad. We had little cash, even for such things as haircuts. But our family had pride and, although we wore hand-me-downs and patched clothes, we always looked well kept, because Dad cut our hair. He even cut his own hair.

Dad had started cutting hair for his father and brothers when he was about 12 or 13. If the job wasn't satisfactory, he might get beat up in the process of a critique by his older brother. So trying to convince me I was lucky, Dad would point out that the haircuts of other kids looked like someone had put a bowl on their head and trimmed around it.

Before electricity, our haircuts always took place on Saturday afternoons. In the summer, Dad cut our hair outside in the cool shade of the trees. In the winter, he did it on the enclosed porch. Always, his "customer" sat on a metal stool saved just for cutting hair.

Dad even had his own barber cloth. It was made of cotton with little strips of color about a quarter-inch wide every *three-quarters of an inch, and it was hemmed at each end. Its tight weave would not let hair even as fine as mine slip through.*

But no matter how tightly I held the cloth around my neck, hair clippings would find an opening and make me itch, then wiggle, which, after what seemed like little patience on my father's part, would result in a whack with the backside of the scissors. Dad wasn't mean; he just was used to working with animals, and tenderness wasn't one of his attributes.

We had a regular barber comb and lever mechanical clippers. The clippers cut hair much more evenly than the scissors did, but the clippers had one awful feature: As more hair went down my neck and my wiggling distracted Dad from squeezing properly, the clippers would bind up in my hair.

The next squeeze would virtually pull my hair out by the roots, prompting me to jump, prompting Dad to get irritated and whack me with the shears, which started the tears rolling, which matted hair to my face, which tickled me something awful, which made me wiggle even worse, which started the cycle over again and again.

Mom always seemed to know when to intercede. She would tell Dad to stop. Then, with a real barber brush she would brush me off, settle me down, shake out the barber cloth, and let Dad resume the awful task.

As a finishing touch, Dad would dash a little talcum from his tin into the brush and brush me down. To this day, I love the smell of talcum, because it signaled the end of a miserable ordeal.

Eventually, we had a little more money and could afford an occasional small luxury, like a town-bought haircut. So while Mom would do her shopping on Saturday night after delivering the cream and eggs and maybe a few chickens to the local produce buyer for some ready cash, Dad would take me to the barbershop at the edge of town.

Usually, by the time we got there, the shop would be full of other farmers, maybe half a dozen men in bib overalls, who gawked at the person coming through the door and then seemed to make a mental note of his place in line for a haircut.

Being a farm boy who rarely was around people, I was timid. It embarrassed me to walk into that little shop and undergo their scrutiny. The barbershop generally was quiet – scary quiet, in fact – except for the hum of the electric clippers or the clatter of the scissors and the click of the barber's comb against them.

It was amazing to watch this professional work. No one seemed to be in pain. There was no crying, not even any talking on the barber's part, except for his occasional "Next" and the pop of the cloth as he shook the hair from it, signaling the end of a customer's service.

It was a frightening experience for me to be next as the barber looked over his glasses to see if I was tall enough to sit in the hydraulic chair or if I would need to sit on the booster board. My voice was changing, which made me self-conscious, so I was happy to say nothing and thrilled I didn't have to use the booster board, anything not to draw attention to myself.

Even though I was just a boy, the barber went about his business efficiently. I hardly felt his touch. And the little piece of cloth he put around my neck, before he pinned on the big cloth that draped graciously over me and the marble-and-leather chair, allowed not one hair to antagonize me. Occasionally he would brush the hair from my face so I'd feel no discomfort.

Before I knew it, he was saying quietly, "Next." I was through.

Consultants and Professionals

The ease with which that barber cut my hair showed me that hiring someone to do a job rather than doing it in-house can be the better alternative. Hire a consultant or a professional when you don't have the staff, the expertise, or the time to work on a problem.

But before you make that decision, consider several things. What is the issue? How frequently is it likely to recur? How long would teaching somebody internally to handle it take? Is having a resident expert worth the expense? Comparatively, how much would hiring an outsider cost? Could a joint team of internal and external people work?

Call In the Experts

Short-term or intermittent issues call for consultants. For example, a problem arose concerning the disposition of chemicals used in our manufacturing process. We don't have a chemist on staff. The problem was relatively minor, compared with all the other problems we handle daily in running a business, so it wasn't something we had time to research. It was a perfect project for an outside consultant.

Before we looked for a consultant, we talked to the overseeing government agencies to see what we had to do to comply with regulations. Equipped with that knowledge, we then could determine which of the consultants we interviewed was qualified to do the project.

Get an expert's help when you're taking on a big new project, or even when you're doing something familiar that depends upon more than your usual expertise. Every time we've expanded our facilities, about half a dozen times now, we've started by getting our ideas on paper far enough along that we can explain what we want. Then we find a professional architect or engineer to finish the plans to our specifications.

Learning new things is part of a manager's daily life, but you don't want to find out something the hard way, such as learning too late your property isn't zoned for the activity you've planned or the building you've designed.

As for taxes, you can't afford not to have a consultant, an accountant. With all the tax programs, tax-credit investments, and other tax oddities, you must have someone who keeps current on the ever-changing regulations and opportunities. Doing your own taxes is a waste of your time, and you can't possibly do as good a job as a professional.

Where to Find Consultants

Some consultants hang out their shingle as a professional and charge you for their services. Other consultants are happy to give you information for nothing. These are the salespeople – the information carriers – who can tell you not only about their products but also about the marketplace of other similar and related products, in hopes you will buy theirs.

When you start to research a problem or a project, look at what is in the market, right on the shelf, then invite sales representatives to present their product to you and tell you how it will fix your problem. Of course, a salesperson's opinion is biased, so you'll want to listen to more than one, but salespeople can educate you quickly on what's available to solve your problem, as well as what criteria to use to develop a solution.

Look for consultants in companies whose products you buy. For instance, the company that sells you casualty insurance probably has loss-control consultants who will help you evaluate your situation. Or, for example, if you want to buy some exotic steel from a Chicago warehouse, their service might include the advice of their resident metallurgist.

Other sources of information, of course, are trade journals and magazines. Not only do you get good advice, but also you find the experts, who might be appropriate consultants for you, and whether organizations exist that could be additional sources of information. Don't overlook others who run businesses similar to yours. And, as I've already said for other reasons, be sure you're a member of the trade organizations pertaining to your industry.

Without the help of independent consultants, we couldn't keep up with all the acts and bills that come along, issuing new mandates for businesses. The advice of those consultants can prevent serious fines. Government agencies themselves, at all levels, are possible sources of consultation services.

Yes, you do have to be concerned that you might open yourself to penalties. But, with some agencies, you're more likely to get a favorable response if you initiate the contact than if you wait for a surprise inspection that results in a violations report. And, after all, through taxes you are paying for their services, whether or not you use them.

The Consulting Team

We have formed a team of consultants for specialties in which we need expertise on a regular basis, such as legal matters, accounting, insurance, and pension plans. One expert in each area does our general ongoing work. For special concerns we go outside this group.

In legal matters, for example, one attorney realistically can't be an expert in all law subspecialties, such as real estate, labor, pension, or incorporation. We wouldn't use our corporate attorney to advise us on our employee stock-ownership program (ESOP), for example. Instead, we encourage our professionals to coordinate selected consultants. It's more effective and much cheaper than risking a penalty for a mistake.

A special word here about your insurance representatives: Treat them like consultants, rather than just salespeople with a product. Use their consulting services to the fullest for expert advice to help you improve your business and cut insurance costs. Hiding information about your business from them only hurts you. Yet, foolishly, people do just that, making adversaries rather than team members of people whose advice could be invaluable.

A friend worked for years as a loss-control specialist. His job was to look for potential problems in businesses his company insured. What he didn't like about his job was discovering things people were trying to hide rather than fix, situations creating risks to which his insurance company hadn't agreed. The result: higher insurance costs because of higher risks.

An Objective Look at Your Business

On many occasions, I've hired "guest consultants," not for any particular problem, but, rather, to critique our company, to give us a fresh perspective. These are people I have known in the business community or about whom I have read, people whose opinions I respect. They have been successful in their own endeavors, which include unusual or difficult experiences.

The backgrounds of these consultants usually have something in common with ours. One individual, for example, ran an engineering firm that designs buildings. We invited him to look at our organization, which designs, engineers, and builds machinery.

We occasionally meet with an evaluating consultant to discuss our business. We want our adviser to respond to what we say, to tell us what he thinks we're doing right and doing wrong. This exercise benefits us tremendously. The consultant might tell us how he handled a problem similar to one we might be confronting. Often, it isn't that he tells us things we don't know; it's that hearing someone we respect confirm our ideas gives us greater confidence to act.

Putting our ideas into words, we ourselves learn more about our company and the way we're managing it. Sometimes these meetings continue over several months. Such consulting services cost thousands of dollars, but the results are well worth the expense to us.

Our ESOP requires that the financial condition of the company be evaluated every year. Even if you don't have an ESOP, I'd recommend this procedure because, for the $3,000 to $4,000 cost, you get an objective estimate of the economic value of your company.

How someone else sees your company is an excellent education. What you believe your company is worth probably is not what a buyer would be willing to pay for it, but by learning how a buyer would look at your company, you discover ways to improve it and to make it worth more.

We have hired an investment banker who sells companies to consult with us on this issue. With experience as a seller's representative, he's been able to give us a good estimate of the company's financial value and ways to improve its value.

The Real Value of Consulting Services

What is a consultant really worth? A more appropriate question is: What is a particular consultant's opinion worth to you? Start by asking a potential consultant how much he would charge to sit down with you and listen to your story. Often, pay is based on availability – the old issue of supply and demand. But some consultants charge twice the fee of others. You have to decide whether you can gain enough from their experience to justify the cost.

Problems arise for which you should put all available money toward finding a solution and applying it immediately. Other problems could go on for years without affecting the bottom line, and you could apply minimal amounts of money toward solving them. The issue is not how much money you should apply toward a problem, but how serious the problem is. So, for a disaster in the making, don't budget consulting fees. Formulas don't work here. When you really need a consultant, get one. Pay what you must to solve the problem.

Manage Your Consultants

Don't waste your consultant's time or yours; know why you want to hire such an adviser. Once you hire, communicate. Tell the person what you expect from the relationship. Above all, don't hold back information.

If you don't trust the individual enough to be honest and open when you talk about your business, find another consultant. Be sure your consultant respects you enough not to say things just because you want to hear them. You need someone who can critically inquire about your company, so you're getting something from the inquiry. That keeps a business growing.

Document conversations. Keep notes on meetings and phone conversations. Write memos to confirm what you understand was said in a conversation concerning critical information.

Don't just turn consultants loose in your company. Outsiders can't replace you. Coming with a different bias, they can't be expected to understand the entire situation. To interpret the facts, they'll need your guidance. For another reason, the reaction of employees toward them will always be far different from the employees' reaction toward you. Besides, consultants are temporary – employees can wait them out.

Don't hire consultants so you can take a nice vacation. I know of a business owner who hired some consultants to come in and manage while he left for some other projects. When he returned, he discovered that, while he was away, his consultants had nearly run the business into the ground, jeopardizing its financial well being to their advantage.

The laissez-faire style of management is risky. Keep track of your consultants. Work with them, inspect their progress. Not only ask for but get interim reports, if circumstances indicate that step. When the buck stops with you, it is you who must exercise due diligence.

Looking for a Contractor

When buying contracting services, there are many considerations, not the least of which is the contractor's reputation and size. Certainly, price is a factor, but not the most important one. Important, too, is the current environment of the marketplace.

For example, when we put up our new building, subcontractors were in short supply. I knew if I picked a contractor who had one sub to do all the tasks – footings, electrical wiring, and so on – I was going to get one busy sub who wouldn't be afraid to quote all the jobs high.

What I wanted was a contractor with access to several subcontractors, so he could get competitive pricing. I also wanted a medium-sized contractor, one for whom we were not the smallest client.

What I didn't consider was my being the general contractor on the project. Subs have allegiance to their general contractor and, especially in the prevailing tight labor market, they wouldn't have given me the time of day.

Chapter 12
Summary

Wle were all at the table for dinner (the noon meal on a farm), when the phone rang three shorts and one long. That was our signal on the party line. Mom answered the phone. It was Joe Nave: "Is Wayne there?"

Of course, he knew Dad was in from the field on this hot July day a few minutes after twelve o'clock. Hanging up, Dad uttered only, "The papers are ready to sign," before he went back to eating his meal as quietly as before.

After dinner, he didn't go into the parlor and lie down on the floor for a cool nap, as he usually did. He went directly outside toward the car, parked in the shade of a tree. I pleaded to go with him. I just wanted something to do other than be a farm boy imprisoned by the same boring chores or whatever else was the whim of my parents. "Oh, let him go," Mom said.

That Dad didn't say no seemed a miracle. He didn't say yes, but the absence of a no was license enough for me to open the car door and jump in. Where were we going? I didn't care. I was going somewhere.

We soon pulled up in front of the Foster Co-op Credit Association, a small community bank in Foster, the town closest to our farm. I followed Dad into the bank, taking care to keep a strong hold on the screen door, with its tight spring, so it wouldn't catch the back of my leg as I stretched up to grab the handle of the big wooden door with my other hand.

That door opened onto a world beyond my imagination. What I was about to see separated me from the farm forever.

We walked directly toward a large marble counter topped with brass. The ceiling was high – higher than any ceiling I had ever seen before, with a huge paddle fan. There were big blinds on the windows of the brick building, and it was cool inside.

Joe was businesslike but friendly: "Hi, Wayne. Who's that with you? Have a seat." He made me comfortable in a great big oak chair. "Here are the papers. I think they are the way we discussed and all in order." Dad moved toward a large desk covered with papers and, after a brief look, started signing. When he was finished, Joe said, "The money is in your account. You can buy the cattle we talked about any time."

We didn't delay and I knew better than to ask for ice cream or pop. I got back into the car for the quiet ride back home, but after what I'd seen at the bank, I couldn't think of anything else except this other world of business. At the first opportunity, I tried to recreate the scene with papers and an impromptu desk in the spare room.

I could never be a farmer after that day, that experience.

Reiteration

Scratching the itch of entrepreneurship is a wonderful way to spend one's life, but there is much to know to make it an enjoyable, productive venture – or, rather, adventure. Not everyone is cut out to own or manage a business, any more than everyone is capable of becoming a computer expert or a professor or a mechanic or a veterinarian or an explorer. Success depends upon several factors, including some important personality traits.

Pride, tenacity, and the ability to learn quickly, of themselves, do not define a successful entrepreneur. But more than other qualities, they provide the basis for the possibility of success. Over them drape the layers of personality an individual seeking fulfillment as an entrepreneur most often possesses. Traits such as proactivity, self-rule, risk taking, and a healthy dose of realism do not guarantee success but certainly tilt the scales toward it.

Just as certain traits contribute to a person's effectiveness in business, so, too, does success depend upon the right reasons and the right ways to choose a particular business. It also depends upon good preparation. Impatience, thinking an opportunity to buy a business will be your only one, and the idea you won't have to answer to anyone are poor reasons to commit your future to any venture.

Prepare for the business you want to buy or start by getting educated. Learn as much as you can about the industry it's in. Take classes. Read the trade magazines. Apprentice yourself to someone already in the business. All are ways to help determine whether owning or managing a business might be appropriate for you.

As in farming, success in business is directly connected to good stewardship. Thinking long term rather than short will guide you toward company-sustaining strategies and practices. Risk is part of any business, but calculate the likely outcome of any risk you take. Be sure the odds are in your favor.

Running a business is about responsibility. Whether a business flourishes or founders, you, ultimately, are the principle reason. As the head of the corporate community of people you assemble, you, more than anyone, set the tone for the kind of group that evolves. Take care when you choose employees. Focus on continually improving the quality of the group. Involve employees in decisions affecting them. Cultivate a positive environment. Nourish your community.

Understanding human nature is a lifelong process. The more you know about it, the better manager you will be. When you hire employees, consider both personality traits and aptitudes. A person might be capable of performing the tasks of a job but ill-suited for the psychological aspects of it. We violate employees when we place them in jobs that violate their personality. So, think about what traits a job requires, and try to fit the job with an individual who has those attributes.

Long-term relationships are vital in building a successful business. It's no secret. Loyal employees, returning customers, dependable vendors, and a supportive public community develop over time. If you focus on the short-term or on only what's in it for you, your business will be like a shallow-rooted tree in a storm. Instead, grow deep roots.

Improved efficiency contributes directly to your profitability. Determine what is inside your "circle of influence" and focus on it. Set priorities in time, effort, and finances. Learn to delegate. Subdue your pride and hire people to cover your deficiencies. It's OK to have weaknesses.

Your business is part of your life. It will express your real values. What is the rationale for your choices? What do you believe in? Keep your philosophy in mind when you make decisions, not rigidly, but with tolerance toward other points of view. Compromise for the greatest good overall.

Urgent situations, even though not necessarily important, drain resources, because they limit your options. If you plan your work and work your plan, you are more apt to get beyond situations that are both vital and urgent to the place where you are able to think, in your own good time, about what is vital but *not* urgent.

Day-to-day operations demand as much time as you want to give them, but you must think about the big picture. Set aside time to develop long-range plans, to set goals. If you expand capability, you will be ready for greater opportunity, and you will further your success.

At the same time, control debt so you can manage during difficult times. Whenever you spend, think about the return on your investment. Are you getting sufficient value for what you are actually paying?

Determine your market. Remember, all customers are not equal. Cultivate good customers. Take care of them. Scrutinize situations that sound too good to be true. Say no to deals that aren't profitable.

Treat your vendors respectfully by being a good customer yourself. But buy; don't be sold. Avoid circumstances that make you feel obligated to a salesperson.

Don't let your business consume your life. Get away from your business regularly. Cultivate avocations. And, especially, set aside time to learn. There is no such thing as too much knowledge.

I wish you good luck and a prosperous life.

References

Fisher, Roger, and Ury, William. *Getting to Yes: Negotiating Agreement Without Giving In.* 2d ed. New York: Penguin Books, 1991.

Gilbreth, Frank B., Jr., and Carey, Ernestine Gilbreth. *Cheaper by the Dozen.* New York: Bantam Books, 1948.

Guralnik, David B., Editor in Chief. *Webster's New World Dictionary of the American Language.* New York: Simon & Schuster, 1980.

Hobbs, Charles R. *Your Time and Your Life.* Chicago, IL: Nightingale-Conant Corporation, 1983.

Merrill, A. Roger. *Connections: Quadrant II Time Management.* Provo, UT: Institute for Principle-Centered Leadership, 1990.

Index